T0065421

Abiding
In the
Secret
Place

A Practical Guide
for Living from
the Presence of God

(First Sequel to Wisdom for Mothers)

Gloria Boakye

WESTBOW
P R E S S®
A DIVISION OF THOMAS NELSON
& ZONDERVAN

WestBow Press books may be ordered through booksellers or by contacting:

WestBow Press
A Division of Thomas Nelson & Zondervan
1663 Liberty Drive
Bloomington, IN 47403
www.westbowpress.com
844-714-3454

ISBN: 978-1-6642-0181-1 (sc)
ISBN: 978-1-6642-0182-8 (e)

Print information available on the last page.

WestBow Press rev. date: 08/28/2020

DEDICATION

I dedicate this book to my three beautiful daughters, Sheryl, Elizabeth, and Josette. Mothering you has taught me so much and seeing you grow into beautiful God loving people gives me the greatest joy.

ACKNOWLEDGEMENT

I give all glory, honour and praise to my Lord and Saviour Jesus Christ, the lover of my soul. I owe every good thing in my life to You Lord.

This book wouldn't be here if not for the enormous encouragement and support of my loving husband, Pastor Joseph Boakye. Thank you for all your support.

I would like to appreciate and honour my spiritual father, Rev. Dr David Antwi. Thank God for his dedicated life of passion and commitment to Christ which is so infectious. I honour you sir.

I honour my spiritual mother, Rev. Awo Antwi, who recognised the gift of writing in me. Thank you for seeing treasure in me and for continually encouraging me to always be my very best and not to settle for less.

The enormous input of Rev.K.T. Bossman and Rev. Mrs. J.E. Bossman in my life will never be forgotten. Thank you for seeing value in me and for the many opportunities you gave me to grow in ministry. I am also grateful to you for showing me the importance of maintaining a healthy family life whilst doing ministry.

My appreciation also goes to Rev. Celia Appiagyei Collins of Rehoboth Foundation. Your exemplary lifestyle of living with passion for the Lord in everyday life continues to inspire me

I also want to thank and honour my biological parents, Mr Prince Kwame Wiafe, and Ms Bridgette Abena Somoa for always being there for me.

My gratitude also goes to my siblings Sandra, Prince, and Kevin. Thank you for believing in me.

I am also grateful for my beautiful friend Mrs Afiba Vanderpuye for her continual support and encouragement. You have proven to be a true friend indeed. Thank you being a righteous influence in my life.

Finally, I would like to thank Mrs Selom Gogo for beautifully editing this book. God richly bless you

FOREWORD

ABIDING IN THE SECRET PLACE

One may find that many sequels to books or movies usually tend to be repetitive and do not offer the reader any new perspective or information from the original.

I must say, that is not so for this book, 'Abiding in the Secret Place' – sequel to 'Wisdom for Mothers'.

In this book, Gloria takes the reader on a journey which continues from where it stopped in the first book, 'Wisdom for Mothers'. It is not a repetition but a continuation.

The book so much captivated me, that I read it from cover to cover, in one sitting, without leaving my desk. The message in the book inspired, motivated and indeed empowered me to arise and run the race of life, knowing that if I made the Almighty God my dwelling, nothing would be impossible for me to achieve.

Gloria expounds on another revelation to the scripture in Psalm 91 which many Christians may not have gained insight into.

If you are a mother, and indeed a parent, anxious about what the future holds for your life and for your children, then this book is definitely the one for you to pick up and read.

It will challenge you to rely solely on God for the strength, wisdom, knowledge, insight and 'know-how' to live life purposefully and guide your children to do the same.

I highly recommend this book for every parent and parent-to-be. Pick up a copy of this book, read it, digest it, apply it to your life you will reap the benefits of 'Abiding in the Secret Place' of the Most High God.

Mrs. Afiba Vanderpuye
Chartered Civil Engineer & Mother to 3 Children

CONTENTS

Safety of Abiding in the Presence of God

It is an undisputable fact that the Word of God is the richest source of hope and life. It is filled with many luxurious promises of abundance, health, and pleasure for every area of life. Can you imagine the reality of experiencing all the promises of God in your life and that of your loved ones? Take a minute to simply imagine the possibilities of living out one of my favourite Bible verses: Psalm 91. See yourself living out the realities of all the promises of this scripture as you read it out to yourself:

Psalm 91, NKJV

He who dwells in the Secret Place of the Most High
Shall abide under the shadow of the Almighty.
² I will say of the LORD, "*He is* my refuge and my fortress;
My God, in Him I will trust."

³ Surely He shall deliver you from the snare of the fowler
And from the perilous pestilence.
⁴ He shall cover you with His feathers,
And under His wings you shall take refuge;
His truth *shall be your* shield and buckler.
⁵ You shall not be afraid of the terror by night,
Nor of the arrow *that* flies by day,

⁶ *Nor* of the pestilence *that* walks in darkness,
Nor of the destruction *that* lays waste at noonday.

⁷ A thousand may fall at your side,
And ten thousand at your right hand;
But it shall not come near you.
⁸ Only with your eyes shall you look,
And see the reward of the wicked.

⁹ Because you have made the LORD, *who is* my refuge,
Even the Most High, your dwelling place,
¹⁰ No evil shall befall you,
Nor shall any plague come near your dwelling;
¹¹ For He shall give His angels charge over you,
To keep you in all your ways.
¹² In *their* hands they shall bear you up,
Lest you dash your foot against a stone.
¹³ You shall tread upon the lion and the cobra,
The young lion and the serpent you shall trample underfoot.

¹⁴ "Because he has set his love upon Me, therefore I will deliver him;
I will set him on high, because he has known My name.
¹⁵ He shall call upon Me, and I will answer him;
I *will be* with him in trouble;
I will deliver him and honour him.
¹⁶ With long life I will satisfy him,
And show him My salvation."

The truth is that all these and more can be yours! The word of God is real and it is for us.

INTRODUCTION

In a world plagued with fear, uncertainty, and chaos, many hearts are fainting, stressed and panicked, not knowing what the future holds. Although the Bible is full of great promises for the believer, many are still kept awake at night, overly concerned about their safety and wellbeing.

A lot of mothers are playing the game of chance hoping that they will be "lucky" somehow; but the Bible clearly states that though perilous times will come in the last days, we, as children of God are not meant to be victims of such circumstances. The Bible provides us with great promises of blessings for every area of our lives.

It is however rather ironic that these beautiful promises tend to be more theoretical than practical to many well-meaning Believers. Could this be the reason why miracles are such a huge topic in many Christian communities? Indeed, if we truly live out the scriptures, our everyday lives will be miraculous even in the midst of turbulent situations (such as the current global pandemic). Miracles will not be occasional and rare occurrences, or emergency interventions in a crisis - we will be living in them daily; they will be our normal lifestyle.

As a committed seeker of God, I have come to know God as real and true to His word. What God says about us in the Bible is true and indeed can be realized right here on earth. Indeed, there are many people just like you and I living out the realities of God's promises right now.

My hunger to seek God has led to a practical experience with God and His Word. I have committed the time to search the scriptures to find out how to live out the Word of God in my everyday life. I want more than a theory. I want to experience His promises for real. It is this quest that has motivated me to write this book. My desire is to help mothers and all Believers to get into a place of living out the Word of God with all authenticity before His presence. This book is about "doing life" with Jesus for real on a daily basis as scripture commands we should do.

As a Christian mother with a vision to glorify God by completing down to the last detail all that He has assigned me to do, I have always strived for excellence and success in every area of my life. However, I quickly accepted the utter futility of my efforts without the help of God. Striving to achieve significant success by relying on my strength just left me exhausted and unfulfilled.

I decided to begin to engage God by establishing a deep and personal relationship with Him not only in my personal Bible Study and Prayer life, but in my daily living.

The responsibilities of motherhood and other commitments which I found laborious and tasking began to unravel as a joyful experience because I ceased to do them in my own strength and began to rely wholly on God.

As believing mothers, we must understand that real success in life cannot be achieved through hard work, planning and personal development alone. The world as we know it has changed and will not return to life as we knew it. We must therefore engage God in every area of our lives going forward and this must start with a proper understanding of who we are as Christian mothers and how to successfully navigate our lives as such.

I have written this book, "Abiding in the Secret Place" as an invitation for you to join me take the most amazing journey into the presence of God and *make that our permanent dwelling place*, where the Lord Himself is our habitation (see Psalm 91:9). It is a glorious place to live, it is a place of rest and peace.

Yes, the world is turbulent and nothing is certain at the moment but, we have a sure promise from the Father that even in these troubling times, those of us who know our God shall be strong and do exploits (see Daniel 11:32). This is our time to shine bright (see Isaiah 60:2, Matthew 5:14). The effect of light is most appreciated in darkness. As the light of a troubled world, we get to shine brightest in these perilous times.

I'll like to invite you to grab a cup of coffee and cuddle up in your sofa or block out all the noise during your commute, as we take this glorious journey into the Secret Place of the Most High as mothers. Let us learn the dynamics of getting there and most importantly, how to STAY there.

Come along with me into the Secret Place of the Most High. I'm sure you will enjoy the ride. Let's get started.

Shalom.

Why I Wrote This Book

A little while ago, after my quiet time, the Lord dropped the words, "the Secret Place of the Most High" in my heart. I realised that this is a portion of scripture from Psalm 91. After studying it, I understood that I was supposed to make the Secret Place of the Most High my permanent dwelling place in order to experience the manifestation of the remaining blessings of this Psalm in my life.

Psalm 91 is a very popular scripture known by many Christians. Its popularity is often based on the promised blessings of protection and greatness it offers. It is also one of the prominent warfare scriptures used by many Christians to claim protection over themselves and their loved ones in times of both physical and spiritual attacks. During the global pandemic of Covid-19, it became the go-to passage for almost every sermon, and a source of strength for Believers all over the world.

Despite the unquestionable potency of this scripture and its popularity amongst many Believers, it is evident that the reality of the blessings within this scripture is not always experienced fully by so many who know and quote this scripture accurately. Could this be because the required conditions for the actualization of the promised blessings are intentionally or unintentionally overlooked or ignored?

The problem can never be God, because "As for God, His way is perfect; The word of the Lord is proven; He is a shield to all who trust in Him" (Psalm 18:30 NKJV). Moreover, Jesus declared that

"Heaven and earth will pass away, but My words will by no means pass away" (Mark 13:31).

The fault, therefore, lies with us.

We are missing something!

Permanent Residence

Before we go further, please ingrain this important point in your heart: *God is calling you into a place of permanent dwelling.* This is not a one-off or occasional experience here and there. This is about habitation, the reality of making the presence of God your constant dwelling place. It requires a posture of conviction and a declaration of intent to commit to this pursuit. Understand that any invitation or command given to you from God comes with the ability to execute it. In other words, if God is calling you to constantly abide in His presence, then He has also given you the power and ability to obey Him.

Obedience

As mothers, our craving for protection and blessings for our children is normal and it shows a healthy passion that reflects Father God's heart which delights in the wellbeing of His children. The Father's heart desires to brood over His children as a hen broods over its little ones (Matthew 23:37). We must, therefore, understand the needed requirements and conditions we must meet to claim these great promises in Psalm 91 and other related promises of God in the Bible.

There is a qualifying factor or condition for the blessing of Psalm 91. This is spelt out in the first verse; we are required to *dwell / remain / stay in the Secret Place of the Most High* so we can then *abide under the shelter of the Almighty*; then the blessings will begin to flow.

This truth is echoed in both Old and New Testament scriptures such as Isaiah 26:3 and Romans 12:2. These verses explain the need to remain fixed on God and to align our thoughts and lives to His word to see Kingdom change and blessings in our lives.

Some instructive scriptures in the Bible are very fundamental and instrumental in seeing the changes and blessings the word of God promises in the life of the believer. Some of these scriptures include Psalm 91:1 (dwelling in the Secret Place), 2 Cor 10:5 (taking every thought captive), Isaiah 26:3 (Keeping our minds stayed on God), Romans 12:2 (renewing our minds), Joshua 1:8 – 10 (meditating and confessing the word), Hebrews 12:2 (looking unto Jesus), and many more.

These scriptures mainly instruct us to take responsibility for our thought life and conform it to God's word so our lives will change from glory to glory. God is serious about His word and we must begin to pattern our lives to obey His holy word so we can see the blessings He has promised us.

God wants all of you

In the past couple of years, I have felt a continual draw into the presence of God. I feel Him calling me into a closer and more intimate walk with him. This draw is not just a call into a set time of prayer and devotion (though that is vital and necessary) but it is more of a call to totally immerse every aspect of my life into God.

I am learning that God wants to do life with His children at every waking moment. He wants to be engaged in everything we do. To put it more conventionally, it appears God wants us to "have church" all the time in every life activity we engage in. I know this is not a common perception of Christianity but in my research in the Bible, I have discovered that God will have nothing less.

He wants it ALL. All of me and All of you too! He wants to be involved in everything all the time.

Responding to this call has led me to encounter God through His word in great and lovely ways. Journeying into the Secret Place of the Most High has not been a perfect one for me but He holds my hands, and every day, as He draws me, I discover depths of Him that are changing my life. God's plans for us are greater, bigger and better than anything we can chase after in our strength.

Saying yes to the call into the Secret Place is a plus to your life because God knows everything about you and your family and He has designed the perfect plan just for you. He also has all the details and strategies required for you to succeed. The Lord knows the best path for you and He knows the way that evil eyes cannot discern. (Job 28:7), a path of safety and sure success just for you.

As you heed to him, you tap into His grace, strength, and wisdom that will help you fulfil your destiny. When you dwell in the Secret Place, you get to feel God's heartbeat, you dream with Him and work with Him as you pursue His calling and assignments for your life. Making the Secret Place your favourite place will put you in a place of advantage.

Safety in the Secret Place

We have all experienced the frustrating feeling of having our daily routines significantly altered or scrapped, our freedoms curtailed by law or forceful governmental suggestion, our work and school lives shut behind closed doors because of the fear of an invisible enemy of Covid-19. We have also experienced many personal trials, traumas and tragedies of varying degrees at different times. There are yet many mountains to climb and obstacles to overcome in the uncertain future, as well. Thus, without the protection of the Lord over you and yours, you can be very vulnerable. Living in proximity with Him will give you a smoother sail into your destiny with every storm and opposition becoming the very instruments that will catapult you into your greatness.

I experienced the safety of the Secret Place in April / May 2020 during the coronavirus pandemic. One of my daughters was diagnosed with hyper inflammatory syndrome – connected to COVID-19. We spent about nine days in ICU and she was on the ventilator for over six days. On the 1st of May, things took a dramatic nose dive when her blood pressure went up from medications given her and doctors prescribed another set of medications to correct the situation. This also failed; meanwhile, her blood pressure went dangerously high whilst her heart rate dropped. It was a scary experience as the doctors were not sure what to do.

Surprisingly during this season, I felt really close to God and knew He had not left me. Whilst by my daughter's bedside, I felt the closeness of God so strongly whenever I closed my eyes; this was comforting and it gave me hope. Yes, as a mother who has been seeking God, I was not expecting this to happen to me and yes, I had questions but I never attributed this to Him, knowing that He is only good and does only good. In a dialogue with God, He pointed out to me that Psalm 91:15 states that He will be with me in trouble and deliver me. That meant that He never promised the absence of trouble but He promised his presence and deliverance in times of trouble. I found this reassurance very comforting.

On the 1st of May, as we prayed and waited, I battled with a strong sense of fear and unbelief. It was almost tangible and foreign to me – very strange. In this state, I called my pastor and other believing friends to support me in prayer. I fell on my face in fear and in tears. Suddenly, I heard the Holy Spirit saying, "get up." As I stood, scriptures started flowing into my heart and I responded by confessing them immediately. One of the verses reminded me that God has not given me the spirit of fear but the spirit of faith. As I continued declaring these scriptures, I felt the fear lifting and faith filling my heart. I continued listening to scriptures and sermons, all the while confessing God's word till, I fell asleep. In the morning, my husband informed me from my daughter's bedside that her condition had stabilised and she was doing well. She continued to improve and we were discharged a few days later.

I appreciate that unfortunately many went through similar circumstances in that time but did not survive. My heart breaks for all parents who lost their children, no matter how old, to the pandemic.

However, in that season, I really understood how profound God's faithfulness and mercies are to dwellers in the Secret Place. I don't know how I could have kept my sanity if God had not been with me giving me peace in the process. My daily habit of meditating on the Word came to my rescue in my time of need, just as Jesus promised that the Holy Spirit will "bring to your remembrance all things that I said to you" (John 14:26 NKJV). It pays to dwell in the Secret Place.

1

THE PROMISE

Psalm 91, according to Jewish tradition, is generally believed to have been penned by Moses, the Servant of God[1]. His unusual experiences and encounters with God from leading the people of Israel out of Egypt through the Red Sea and the miraculous experiences in the wilderness earned him the rich honour of knowing God in depths like no other human. Psalm 91 was therefore birthed from the experiential knowledge of the total protection, provision and above all, intimacy with God, by a man who talked with God face to face.

Amid immense suffering and death, Moses experienced God's protection, provision, and comfort. Further, the proximity that Joshua and Caleb had to Moses allowed them to also see the goodness of God in the same fashion. Joshua then duplicated the same level of obedience and closeness to God, which ultimately led to him having tremendous success in his leadership of the people of Israel, because he and Caleb followed the Lord fully.

DON'T SKIP THE INSTRUCTIONS

Psalm 91 is a remarkably powerful and beautiful Psalm vividly depicting the faithfulness and goodness of God to all who make Him their shelter. Many Christians love to quote and use Psalm 91,

---

[1] www.Biblestudytools.com

usually in times of crisis, or simply to claim the promise of protection from evil.

Ironically, the popularity of this Psalm does not match the reality of the promised blessings in the lives of many Believers who know and quote it. I believe the reason for the lack of manifestation is due to a missed instruction in verse 1 where we are asked to dwell in the Secret Place.

Instead of learning *how* to live out the word, many people simply skip the instructions and jump right to the promised blessings and spend their lives confessing and declaring them. Unfortunately, because the precedent conditions are ignored, the confessions deliver no results. Things don't work by chance in the Kingdom of God. We must adhere to God's standards if we want His blessings. That is God's way; it is not an unreasonable demand.

"He that dwells in the Secret Place of the Most High shall abide under the shadow of the Almighty" (Psalm 91:1 NKJV).

The verse contains a clear instruction and a qualifying factor for the blessings that follow. It is important to understand that you simply cannot ignore the instruction and expect the blessing to manifest in your life. Without dwelling in the Secret Place, all the remaining verses of Psalm 91 are void; it just won't show up in your life no matter how many times you confess it. There is, therefore, the need for you to understand clearly what this Secret Place is and how to dwell there.

The Scriptures are the only authentic source for explaining Scripture, so I will endeavour to use the Scriptures by the help of the Spirit to help us as mothers, find and understand the Secret Place and learn how to dwell there as God instructs us to. If there is such a place of abundant blessing and total protection from evil, then I definitely want that to be my "home".

You Can Do It Because He Has Made Grace Available To You

God's commands are not burdensome because according to 1 John 5:4, "who/whatsoever is born of God overcomes the world." He has given you the capacity to obey Him through His abiding Spirit within you as a believer in Jesus Christ. In other words, you can do this; yes, you can! By the help and strength of the Holy Spirit who is resident in you, you can obey the Lord and do His will. Say Amen!

John 1:12 says that those who receive and believe in Jesus have been given the power to be sons of God. In God's eyes, you are as powerful as Jesus and all things are possible for you (if you believe). You only need to grow into this reality through the renewing of your mind (Romans 12:2).

Engage your mindset

The Secret Place life is a life that allows the manifestation and invasion of heaven in all earthly affairs; the permeation of the Kingdom in every facet of life. It goes beyond orthodox Christianity that is normally exhibited by a life of segmentation and separation of the secular from the spiritual.

It is walking before the Lord 24/7 and doing all things as unto the Lord and for His glory.

The Secret Place is the manifestation of Psalm 16:8 NKJV "I have set the LORD always before me; Because *He is* at my right hand I shall not be moved" and Psalm 73:28 - NASB "But as for me, the nearness of God is my good; I have made the Lord GOD my refuge, That I may tell of all Your works" and Isaiah 26:3 NKJV "You will keep him in perfect peace, Whose mind is stayed on You, Because he trusts in You". Also Joshua 1:8-9 echoes this point of staying close to the Lord by meditating on His word day and night.

In the new testament, the concept of the Secret Place is further echoed in Romans 12:2 where Believers are instructed to be transformed by renewing our minds. Transformation means change, and this change conforms to the reign and rule of the King of glory. The transformation from mere earthly living into living the higher life of heaven on earth, as taught by Jesus in what has become known as the Lord's prayer in Matthew 6:10, "Your kingdom come. Your will be done On earth as it is in heaven.."

In Proverbs 23:7NKJV, the Bible tells us that the essence of a man is the same as his thoughts, "For as he thinks in his heart, so is he…."

If we renew our minds with the Word of God, our thoughts will become Kingdom thoughts and so will our lives be; we will be Kingdom people for real, operating with Kingdom realities, seated in heavenly places far above all the forces of darkness and taking dominion on earth as God commanded us to do in the beginning (Genesis 1:28).

For such a person, no weapon formed against you shall prosper for you are not a mere man! Indeed, according to Psalm 91, when we will DWELL in the Secret Place, preservation and blessing will be our portion! Praise the Lord!

There are many blessings and great feats to achieve in Christ but God requires that we DWELL in the Secret Place, that is IN HIM. Jesus stated in John 15 that we have to abide in the Vine if we are to be fruitful and avoid withering. It is God's will to bless and to protect us and He has given us what it takes to live the Kingdom life. It is now up to us to believe, and receive this by faith. We will go deeper into mindset in Chapter 8.

PRACTICAL RESPONSIBILITY

It should be clear by now that for you to enjoy the Secret Place, there is a human responsibility on your part. Yes, as Christians, we have been blessed with ALL spiritual blessings in the heavenly places (Ephesians 1:3) ; however, there are some practical things to add to your faith to ensure you realise all these spiritual blessings here on earth. In other words, the blessing and goodness of God for the believer is already secured and available but to possess them and get them to be manifested in earthly realms, you have a responsibility do some faith works.

The Christian walk is a partnership. We partner with God in the fulfilment of our assignment. As my pastor, Rev. David Antwi says, "the faith that makes God absolutely responsible is an irresponsible faith". We are to co-labour with God and not just sit and wait for manna to fall from heaven.

God has done His part and we have to respond in faith and obedience and do our part.

2

WHERE IS THE SECRET PLACE?

In Psalm 91:1, we are called to come and dwell in a place called the Secret Place of the Most High.

This then brings us to the question, what and where is this Secret Place?

The Hebrew word used here for the Secret Place is "*sether*" and it means "*covering and hiding place*". Thus, it can be read, "he who dwells under the covering or hiding place of the Most High, shall abide under the shadow of the Almighty."

Dwelling in the Secret Place is, therefore, a spiritual posture of placing yourself constantly under the covering and hiding place of God.

It connotes close proximity to God which can only occur through relationship. This was seen in the lives of some prominent people in the Bible such as David, the king of Israel Moses, the servant of God, and ultimately Jesus Christ, the Son of God.

The Bible talks about Enoch walking so close to God that God just took him away without him experiencing death. It is also written that Joshua would linger in the Tabernacle after everyone had left. He just enjoyed the presence of God. His close walk and service to Moses allowed him proximity to God just like Moses hence Joshua too experienced the blessing and protection of the Secret Place which resulted in him having 100% success and leaving a legacy of greatness after his death. As for Moses, it is written of him that he saw God face to face. He knew the blessing of the Secret Place so well.

The Law in the Old testament is an inferior covenant to the New covenant you have in Christ. Thus, you are in a better position to dwell under God's covering than Moses.

Your access point into the Secret Place is Christ because the Bible tells us in John 14:6, that Jesus is the Way to the Father. The Secret Place is now accessible to only born-again Christians. Without Christ, you cannot make your way into His presence. Christ is the only way into the Secret Place.

Apart from Biblical characters, many have also succeeded in staying in the Secret Place. Amongst such is the famous Brother Lawrence (author of *The Practice of the Presence of God*) who walked in such consciousness of the Lord that though he was not rich and glamourous, he touched so many people because God's presence was on him.

Having established the importance of dwelling in the Secret Place, it becomes necessary for us to find out what the Bible says the Secret Place is and how we can practically dwell there permanently.

Many Christians are sincere and willing to do the right things but sometimes many simply don't know how to do it. There is a lot of knowledge about what to do but I must say, the practical application or the 'how-to' is very much missing in many contexts. God never leaves us clueless on how to do what He commands us to do. We must delve a bit deeper into the Word of God to find out more about the Secret Place of the Most High.

A clear and practical depiction of what the Secret Place is will help you find a biblical guide or map in navigating your way into this precious place and staying there. Just as in real life, you cannot go to a place you do not know, you certainly can't abide or dwell in a spiritual place you cannot navigate to.

THE SECRET PLACE IS THE PRESENCE OF GOD

The Secret Place of the Most High refers to the presence of God. It indicates not only the manifest presence but the consciousness of His presence in everyday living as stated in Proverbs 3:6 which advises that, "in all your ways acknowledge Him, and He shall direct your paths." When we develop a conscious awareness of His presence with us all the time, we dwell in the Secret Place.

Psalm 31:20 NKJV also refers to the presence of God as the Secret Place. Here, the Secret Place of His presence is described as a place of refuge from evil:

"You shall hide them in the secret place of Your
presence From the plots of man; You shall keep them
secretly in a pavilion From the strife of tongues."

Whenever the presence of God is mentioned in scriptures, it is good news for God lovers but dangerous for evil.

God's presence always blesses and preserves His people from their enemies.

In the Amplified and The Passion versions, Psalm 91:1 states that the person in the Secret Place is enthroned under the shadow of Shadai. This links two scriptures: Songs of Songs 2:3 TPT, "… Sitting under his grace-shadow, I blossom in his shade, enjoying the sweet taste of his pleasant, delicious fruit, resting with delight where his glory never fades" and Ephesians 2:6 NKJV; "and raised *us* up together, and made *us* sit together in the heavenly *places* in Christ Jesus,." Other scriptures that depict the Secret Place as the presence of God include the following:

Psalm 32:27 NKJV:

"You *are* my hiding place; You shall preserve me from trouble; You shall surround me with songs of deliverance. Selah

Psalm 119:114 NKJV:

"You are my hiding place and my shield; I wait for Your word".

Psalm 61:3 NKJV:

"For You have been a refuge for me, A tower of strength against the enemy"

Deuteronomy 33:27 NKJV:

"The eternal God is a dwelling place, And underneath are the everlasting arms; And He drove out the enemy from before you, And said, 'Destroy!'

The presence of God is the Secret Place, a place of blessing and refuge from all evil.

THE SECRET PLACE IS "IN HIM"

As explained earlier, the Secret Place is a place of proximity that is only accessible to born-again Christians.

This is because the Bible tells us clearly that no one can get to know or draw close to God without Christ. He is the only Way. The Secret Place is, therefore, a positional place "in Him". In the Old Testament, the Law was the way to God but after the cross, Jesus Christ is the only Way!

Access to Christ makes limitless favour available to the believer, including all the blessings promised in Psalm 91; for in Him all the promises of God are yes and amen (2 Corinthians 1.20). In Christ, you are positionally seated in the heavenly places with Christ and are joint-heirs with Him. All things are yours in Christ including access to the Holy of Holies where deep intimate fellowship with God occurs. Christ makes it possible for us to dwell in the Secret Place.

Though the spiritual position of the believer is secured by the blood of Jesus, the actual physical manifestation of the benefits that accompany salvation requires intentional effort in enforcing these heavenly realities on earth through faith accompanied by good works.

Despite all the promises made to Believers in Christ, it is a shame that many Christians still live defeated low lives.

This is not because God's promises are not true but rather the human responsibility necessary for the manifestation of the promises are often ignored, hence, many only know the promises of God in a theoretical sense rather than experientially.

As a believing mother, you have access to the Secret Place to enjoy sweet fellowship with God and to access all the blessings that come with it. There is however a human responsibility on your part to make this a reality in your life. The Bible tells us to draw near to God and He will draw near to us.

JESUS, OUR PERFECT EXAMPLE

Jesus, as Bill Johnson accurately states in his book *Jesus Christ is Perfect Theology* is indeed perfect theology and also our perfect example of living in the Secret Place of the Most High. There is much to say about Jesus but I will focus on just a couple of points to show that Jesus was a dweller in the Secret Place.

First of all, we must understand that though Jesus was fully God, He submitted Himself to all the limitations of man to the point that in His own words, He could "do nothing" without the Holy Spirit (John 5:30). No works of His was recorded before His baptism and the coming of the Spirit upon Him. As Believers, we are also in the same place, helpless without the Spirit.

Moreover, Jesus had unhindered access to the Father because He was sinless. As Believers in Jesus Christ, we have been cleansed by his blood so we have peace with God. Sin is history; hence we can boldly approach and dwell in God's presence just as Jesus did.

Secondly, Jesus only did what He saw the Father do. He was in constant touch with the Father and simply duplicated what was happening in heaven. To help us do the same, Jesus taught us to pray "Your kingdom come. Your will be done On earth as *it is* in heave" (Matthew 6:10 NKJV). He has positioned us in Him to do just as He did.

Throughout the gospel, it is recorded that Jesus spent quality time praying. He will rise early in the morning, go to a secluded place and pray. Conversations with the Father was a high priority for Jesus and He invested heavily in that.

This is Kingdom living and we can do the same.

It is not far-fetched. If we can embrace salvation, then we can take all that comes with it for He has saved us to the uttermost (Hebrews 7:25).

Heaven's realities can be ours too just us it was for Jesus.

Another beautiful example of Jesus relating with the Father in a practical authentic way is the scene in Gethsemane. This is one of my favourite examples of Jesus because it gives me hope to know that I can be myself before the Father; there is no need to pretend or play strong. It is not necessary. God knows everything and He wants us to be real and true to Him. He desires truth in the heart.

At Gethsemane, Jesus cried out to the Father for help in a moment of weakness, and we see the swift response He received (Luke 22:39-43). Please take a moment to meditate on this scripture and picture the scene. Jesus, who knew exactly what He came on earth to do right from His youth, was asking the Father to change the plan if it was His will. This shows an authentic relationship of honesty and transparency between the Father and Jesus. There is absolutely no pretence; He acknowledged that it was hard - and contrary to the beliefs and perceptions of so many Christians, God was not angry but rather responded by pouring sufficient grace and strength for Jesus to accomplish His will.

Walking with God with such transparency and openness is so beautiful. You are also supposed to build and maintain the same level of openness and authenticity in your relationship with God. He will not judge you but rather help you when you are weak.

You must allow the truth that God is for you and that He is a good God to sink deep in your heart. That way, you will never be afraid to approach Him with anything at any time, knowing and being convinced that He has your best interest at heart.

This posture of heart is however not a license to take the goodness of God for granted or abuse His grace God. I am not talking about hyper-grace or hiding behind the mercy and goodness of God to sin. No! I am talking about sincerity and a true desire to live for God by relying on His grace and strength.

Remember, grace is not only unmerited favour but also empowerment to do the impossible which includes living a righteous life!

3

CONTINUAL CONSCIOUSNESS OF WHO YOU ARE IN CHRIST

Abiding in the Secret Place requires acknowledging who you are in Christ, what He has done for you, and enforcing it by faith.

In practical terms, dwelling in the Secret Place is staying in the continual consciousness of who you are in Christ, believing the finished work of Christ, agreeing with God and engaging the covenant of the blood of Jesus and enforcing the realities of being "in Him" daily. It is actualizing the realities of walking constantly in the presence of God and activating all the benefits and transformational powers therein. As a mother, I ensure I enforce the realities of who I am in Christ daily through confessions and prayers (more on that later).

YOU ARE A CITIZEN OF HEAVEN

When you accepted Jesus as your saviour, you became a citizen of heaven. This is a Bible fact that you need to embrace as a reality in your daily life: *"Now, therefore, you are no longer strangers and foreigners, but fellow citizens with the saints and members of the household of God,"* (Ephesians 2:19 NKJV).

The Christian life is not only physical but also spiritual. This means you cannot live successfully without the active involvement and help of God. Indeed, it is impossible to achieve anything that pleases God without engaging Him in the process through faith.

This is because as a Christian, you are not just an earthly being or citizen but you have also obtained legal citizenship in heaven through the precious blood of Jesus. You have now obtained the higher and privileged status of a dearly loved child of God and are also a fellow member of God's household through Christ Jesus our Lord! Glory to God!

Not only do you live in heaven whilst still on earth but you are also a member of the heavenly royal family and live in God's palace! This is too glorious! Knowing this truth implies that you understand the dynamics of life in the Kingdom of God and live in agreement with heaven's systems of operation or as the Bible puts it, the operation of God's economy (1 Timothy 1.4).

As a citizen of heaven, the Bible describes you as God's own special one and states that all creation is waiting for you to exhibit who you really are so nature can also be liberated from bondage (Romans 8.19). This implies that when Christians express themselves as such, it brings liberation to even nature.

The realities of these truths, however, cannot be experienced if you don't put on the heavenly mindset (the mind of Christ), follow the protocols of the Kingdom, and operate with Kingdom strategies.

As a believing mother, you are no longer who you used to be and so the newness of life must reflect in the way you think and act. This demands a shift in your mindset and approach to life in accordance with the standards of the Kingdom of God.

4

WITHOUT GOD, YOU CAN DO NO PARENTING

I strongly believe that parenting requires an intimate knowledge of God's mind for our children if we are to be successful at 'training them up in the way they should go' (Proverbs 22:6). God has a specific path for every child. A mother can only discover this path when she is intimate with God enough to hear Him speak to her. Walking with God intimately opens you up to His intents and plans that are only revealed by His Spirit.

Moreover, as a parent, you are limited in the extent of your influence in the lives of your children. Soon, they will be away from your protective wings and it is only your trust in God that will give you the peace you need when that time comes. If you walk close enough to the Lord who knows all things and has all power, you can be confident of safety in every sense for yourself and all your loved ones.

THE SOURCE OF REAL SUCCESS

In striving to be my best in every way, I have come to discover that the source of real success for a believing mother with a vision is God Himself. He has proven to be my strength, inspiration, and protection all the time. Without Him, I can do nothing but with Him absolutely nothing is impossible!

It is my unwavering conviction that God is the only source of real success. All attempts at achieving great heights without Him are futile and meaningless. The wise mother will therefore maintain a strong connection with God and draw strength and grace from Him continually.

PRIORITISE PRAYER AND BIBLE STUDY

The question you may ask is, "is intimacy with God necessary for busy mothers?" After all, where is the time to sit and spend lots of time in prayer and Bible study? As a mother with a vision, my desire for achievement and excellence keeps on increasing and sometimes keeping up with the fast-paced life and multi-level responsibilities can be challenging.

I have come to realise that there is always a huge temptation to skip prayer and rather attend to the seemingly 'more important things.' Guaranteed, this approach always proves disastrous. I have come to understand that the more I have to do, the more I actually have to pray and the more I better wait and hear clearly from God before I take any step. I spend time with God not because I have a lot of time to spare but rather, because I don't want to waste time. Failing to spend time with God is planning to waste time.

When you realise how limited and handicapped you are without God, you will understand the truth and fact that you just can't afford to do life without Jesus (John 15:5). Putting God first in your life and engaging Him in everything is a stance of humility that invites the help and grace of God in great measures.

HUMILITY ATTRACTS GRACE

In Songs of Songs 1:5, The Shulamite woman (representing the church) acknowledges her weaknesses and the Bridegroom (Christ) tells her how much He still loves her. This truth is also echoed in the New Testament when James stated in James 4:6 NKJV, "But He gives more grace. Therefore, He says: "God resists the proud, but gives grace to the humble." Walking with God intimately is a posture of humility that qualifies you for more grace.

I understand why some mothers may think this is such an unachievable feat but wait a minute; I am a wife, a mother of 3 girls who are still young (my youngest is 5 years old and my eldest is 13 as at the writing of this book), I work part-time, serve in the ministry, and run a business. I understand the word "busy"! Nevertheless, I consider spending time with God top priority because without Him, I can do nothing. Life is more overwhelming without Jesus. You can also ease your burden if you involve Jesus more actively in your daily life.

If you desire to develop a strong uncompromising lifestyle of fellowship with God, I promise you that this is possible. It is not a religious effort of beating yourself to spend hours in prayer before starting your day but rather a walk of love with the Father, Son and the Holy Ghost and leaning into Him for strength at every waking moment.

I have many dreams and I desire to do so much to the glory of God. This makes it imperative for me to walk with God even more closely so I can decipher which desire is from Him, what to do, how, when and also receive all the dynamics and strategies needed for accomplishing these things with Him and for His glory.

5

MOTHERING WITH GOD

Mothering comes with the reverent responsibility of stewarding the success of another person and the burden can be heavy if you attempt to carry it all by yourself. Influencing someone involves many dynamics and even the best-skilled influencers are still not able to change a heart, the core instrument of enduring change that reflects in a lifestyle.

Without God's help, our best attempts at nurturing and guiding our children towards a successful life could lead them away from their God-given destiny, hence capping their potential. You can never have better than God's best for you. Such misdirected efforts have led to many "successful" individuals who live unfulfilled and miserable lives. Many doctors were meant to be lawyers, many pastors who were meant to be businessmen, many businessmen and women were called to preach the gospel; the list can go on and on. It is sad to say that our society is in a mess of mixed up roles and responsibilities. Without God's help and guidance in our parenting, all we can produce is confusion and chaos.

YEARN FOR GOD'S PERFECT WILL

Mum, remember that your job is not only physical because life is more spiritual than just tangible / natural. You need the supernatural input and help of God otherwise you can easily miss it. As my pastor, Rev. Awo Antwi emphasized in her message, *Mothering for the Next Generation*, partnering with God to co-labour with Him in raising your children will be to your advantage.

As a believing mother, I am very interested in staying in the will of God; hence, what God thinks and says about me and my family matters greatly to me. God's opinion and direction for your life should matter to you too if you are a child of God.

I want to succeed, but I want to have my success in God. I want to please Him in what I do and I want God's best for my children and family, too.

I don't think we can have it any better than God's best for us.

If you also want God's best for you and yours, then determine in your heart to walk closely with Him so you can know His heartbeat and grasp His mind for your life, and for your family.

I have always been interested in knowing *how things work in the Kingdom of God,* hence I study with a curious mind asking how to get things done.

It is an honour to share my journey into the Secret Place with you. I do not consider myself to have attained perfection in abiding in the Secret Place but my hunger for more of God continues to increase as I keep on seeking Him and He keeps drawing me closer to His heart, where I want to dwell. The journey into the Secret Place and doing life with God is a continual learning process. I don't think we can ever arrive "there" here on earth because the more we know Him, the more we discover. The closer we draw to Him, the more we desire to get even closer and it is a beautiful continual journey into MORE and MORE and MORE of Him.

It is a satisfying quest that never seems to end. You get satisfied being with Him but somehow, at the same time, you get hungrier for even more of Him. In natural terms, it could be compared to the taste of a delicious meal that creates a memory and a yearning for more.

The quest and journey into the Secret Place will create in you a holy desire and hunger for more of God and His presence. It seems that is how God has created it to be.

Living in the Secret Place makes it possible to see into God and engage Him in every facet and aspect of our lives as mothers. As we live close to our Maker, His help, blessings, and protections will also not be far from us. He has promised not to withhold any good thing from us, so it is right to expect good from our God who is only good (Psalm 73).

The four living creatures who see God daily in heaven never stop worshipping Him, declaring his holiness. They do this day and night (Revelations 4:8). Could this be because they can't exhaust nor comprehend the Eternal Glorious God?

GOD IS CALLING YOU TO HIMSELF

As we get closer to God, He will ignite a fire in our hearts. God has committed Himself to initiate a love affair with us (John 6:44, Psalm 80:18, John 15:5). He is the One who indeed sparks the fire of desire and quest in our hearts for more of Him, but we must respond and ensure we keep that fire burning. In Leviticus 6:12, God told His people to ensure that the fire on the altar (in our case, it is the altar of our hearts) must constantly stay ablaze and ensure it never goes out.

"And the fire on the altar shall be kept burning on it; it shall not be put out..." (Leviticus 6:12NKJV).

The draw and desire for God you feel are from Him, He is calling you to Himself. No one can go to God unless the Father draws Him. You are privileged because He is drawing you. It is a "God thing" and must be greatly valued, treasured, nurtured and protected. You have to respond with all delight, diligence, and reverence. Respond with awe and holy haste. Heed to the cry in your heart for more of God and fall at His feet and say "yes" to Him. This is how to keep the fire of love burning. He is worthy of it all. In

His presence, there is fullness of joy and at His right-hand pleasures forevermore (Psalm 16:11).

This is your call to come daily into His presence and live your life from this place of power and glory. But how should you respond to this call? As a fellow seeker of His presence, I understand the confusion and disappointment that can occur when you know the need and desire something better but you honestly don't know HOW TO DO IT! It can be so frustrating so I will now delve into some truths that I have discovered from the Word of God as tools and road maps into the Secret Place.

A MOTHER IN THE SECRET PLACE

As a mother, you will enjoy a glorious life when you maintain a lovely relationship with Jesus and dwell in the Secret Place all the time. Imagine staying constantly in touch with the Lord, always enjoying the glory of sweet fellowship, His promised covering and protection, and all the many other benefits. Let us take a look at a few of these.

STRENGTH

I have realised that as a mother, I am in constant need of strength. Mothers exert a lot of physical, emotional and spiritual strength as we go about our daily activities caring, correcting, protecting, managing, teaching and fulfilling other duties as mothers, wives, workers, ministers, etc.

As a mother, you usually have to multitask, which requires that you engage your body, spirit, and emotions at the same time. Even after you have taken your little children to school, your heart is still connected to them. You may spend time either praying for them or simply ready to meet needs that may come from school. At the same time, you may have to tidy up your house, go shopping, or go to work. It takes a lot of energy and strength to do these things with a good attitude. Wives also have to pay attention to their husbands' various needs.

You need the strength of God to succeed as a mother; otherwise, you will break down; which is, unfortunately, the story in many homes. As a believing mother, you can find strength in the Secret Place.

Living in the Secret Place is living in the presence of God where your weaknesses fade away. Walking closely with God refreshes you because you don't take on the unnecessary burdens and stresses of life that strip you of strength. Abiding in the Secret Place means you can easily cast your cares on the Lord to take the load off you as you exchange your stress for His rest. Glory to His holy name.

Life in the Secret Place is also a life of divine joy that is a source divine strength because the Bible says, "… the joy of the LORD is your strength."" (Nehemiah 8:10, Palm 16:11 NKJV).

Walking closely with God empowers you to triumph over every seemingly insurmountable challenge that may come your way in the day.

Like the Psalmist, you can also say that by your God you can run through every troop and leap over every wall of opposition that you may encounter (Psalm 18:29).

Indeed, mothers abiding in the Secret Place receive great strength from the Lord for the fulfilment of their daily assignments.

WISDOM

The Bible says in Proverbs 4:7 that wisdom is the principal thing. A mother needs wisdom as the principal element for her success in life.

Further, the Bible also states in Proverbs 14:1 and Proverbs 24:3 that it takes wisdom to build a house or home.

As a mother, you are a builder; you are building your home and your family and the future God has for you. Without the wisdom of God, you can't succeed in this endeavour.

Since dwelling in the Secret Place is dwelling in Christ and Christ is the wisdom of God (1 Corinthians 1:24) then dwelling in the Secret Place, implies dwelling in the wisdom of Christ.

Therefore, as a mother living in the Secret Place you have access to the wisdom of God all the time. You don't have to make foolish decisions when you are walking with God.

Simply ask Him for wisdom before making any decision. His wisdom is readily available to all who are in Him. Dwelling in the Secret Place will make you a wise mother as you tap into the wisdom of God.

INTERCESSION

It is a beautiful privilege when you can take the needs of others before God and petition Him for answers. In the Secret Place, a mother is not only close to God but enjoys a relationship that affords her the honour of seeking Him for the needs of others.

Moses's intercession for the rebellious children of Israel is a great example of how God can have mercy on people who didn't even deserve His mercies. As you abide in the Secret Place, you get to intercede for your family, friends, neighbours, and for communities and nations. God states in His word that if He can find an intercessor, He will intervene in the affairs of men (Ezekiel 22:30). As a mother in the Secret Place, you are also positioned to play the role of an intercessor and as you do so, you will see God's rule permeate your home, neighbours and community.

A person in right relationship with God has the honour of contacting the grace and mercies of the One who has all the answers to life's problems. In the Secret Place, there is no need to worry because you can pray and have God intervene in all situations in accordance with His will for His glory.

In the Lord's prayer, Jesus taught us to say "…our Father…" (Matthew 9:6 NKJV) This implies that we are a family. Prayer is not just about your needs but about others, too. Always present the needs of other people every time you go into prayer. Pray for your children, your husband, siblings, friends, leaders, pastors, neighbourhood, city, and even other nations and situations that may not affect you directly. The Lord is near unto all who call upon Him in truth (Psalm 145:18).

PURE JOY AND BLISS

Have you encountered the presence of God? It is quite difficult to accurately describe it in words; it is sheer bliss, contentment and inexplicable joy. You feel like this is what you were made for.

Although dwelling in the Secret Place does not mean constant euphoria, it positions you for encounters with the Lord in some special ways that not only change your life but the impression and memory can last a lifetime. Such encounters take God from the realm of theory into tangibility. It is just beautiful.

Abiding in the Secret Place is abiding in His presence where there is fullness of joy. Challenging times cannot steal your joy because the Lord is your portion and the joy of your life.

ACCESS GOD'S MIND AND DIRECTION FOR YOUR FAMILY

A successful mother is the one who lives out God's plan for her life. Jesus stated in John 17:4 that He glorified God by completing down to the last detail all that He assigned Him to do on earth. Jesus is the ultimate model of a life well lived and He set the standard for us.

Jeremiah 29:11 reveals that God has a plan for us. You were created with an assignment that suits your make-up in every sense. It is your responsibility to seek out this plan of God so you can fulfil it.

Dwelling in the Secret Place allows you to buy into the mind of God for your life and that of your family to enable you fulfil your destinies.

Doing life in the Secret Place moves you away from the game

of chance into the place of purpose where you get to live out God's plan for your life.

God promises to reveal His secrets to those who seek Him.

His plans for you are great and available, but it is those who make Him their dwelling place who get to live out this glorious intention and plan of God in its fullness.

This is because God has committed Himself to order the steps of the righteous; those who acknowledge Him in all their ways. In effect, it is only a dweller in that Secret Place who would be able to acknowledge God in *all* their ways.

A revelation of God's plans, ways, secrets, directions, and paths and much more are all available to dwellers in the Secret Place.

As a mother, always engage God in your decision-making ensuring that you are attentive to His promptings and whispers. This will save you many heartaches and bring you into great blessings.

An Instrument of God

It is only normal for God to use those who love Him.

God chose Joshua to succeed Moses because of Joshua's loyalty not only to Moses but to God.

He loved God's presence and lingered in the house of God after everyone had left (Exodus 33:11). Lovers of God, dwellers in the Secret Place carry the heartbeat of God and so it is easier for them to do things God's way. This positions them well as possible instruments of God.

In the Secret Place, you get to prepare for ministry and service.

6

Salvation Leads into the Secret Place

We have established that the Secret Place is "In Him" and it is also the presence of God. Thus, dwelling in the Secret Place is living in a loving relationship with the God-head through Christ in a continual thriving fellowship.

This implies that you cannot abide in the Secret Place without access to God through a legitimate relationship.

Salvation

The Bible tells us that no one can go before God except through Jesus Christ. Jesus Himself made this profound declaration to make this point clear when He stated:

"...I am the way, the truth, and the life. No one comes to the Father except through Me." (John 14:6 NKJV).

Jesus is the only way to the Father.

If you don't know Jesus as your Lord and saviour, then I will like to take this opportunity to invite you to receive Him into your life as your saviour today. The Bible tells us that "as many as received Him, He gave them the power to become sons of God" (John 1:12 NKJV). This promise still stands for all who will believe and receive Jesus today.

The Bible also says that "for all have sinned and fallen short of the glory of God" (Romans 3:23 NKJV). Because of the sin of Adam, all humanity have become sinful in nature and are hopeless, and on their way to hell (Ephesians 2:12). But God, in His love, mercy and determination to maintain His original intent and plan for man provided a way out, an opportunity for a fresh start, a second chance to make it right (John 3:14-16).

Getting right with God is not through some religious self-induced acts of righteousness but by simply putting your trust in Christ and receiving His finished work on the cross. God sent Him to take our place so that the condemnation that was due us because of sin was placed on Him. In return He gave His righteousness to all who believe in Him and this righteousness becomes our access into the presence of God, the Secret Place of the Most High.

God gives us salvation by grace and we receive it through faith. It is the gift of God to all who will believe and receive Jesus Christ (Ephesians 2:8-9, Romans 10:9).

If you believe in your heart that Jesus is the Son of God and that God sent Him to come on earth and to die for your sin and on the third day He resurrected for our righteousness, then please say the following prayer now:

Jesus, I believe You are the Son of God.
I believe you died for my sin and rose again on the third day for my salvation.
I confess that I am a sinner.
I repent of my sins and ask you to forgive me.
I invite You into my heart and my life today to be my Lord and saviour.
Please fill me with your Holy Spirit now and help me live my life wholly for your glory every day.
I believe I am saved and filled with your Spirit. Thank you, Jesus. Amen.

If you prayed the above prayer with sincerity and honesty, then you are now born again and have become a legitimate child of God.

You are now a member of God's own family (Ephesians 2:19), all of heaven's resources and blessings are available to you (Ephesians 1:3). You have become a joint heir with Christ and are now seated with Him in the heavenly places (Romans 8:17, Ephesians 2:6). This is indeed your reality!

Your position in Christ is guaranteed because you are sealed with the Spirit of God and your place in heaven is secured (Ephesians 1:13).

After Salvation, What Next?

As a child of God, in the realm of the spirit, you are perfect and complete. However, the realities of this glorious life in the spirit are to be manifested here on earth through a partnership with God in working out your salvation with fear and trembling (Philippians 2:12). This simply means that what you have experienced in the spirit has to be worked into manifestation in the physical realm.

There is an assignment from God on your life. He has called you for a purpose. It is your responsibility to now discover and spend the rest of your life on earth fulfilling this assignment/calling (Jeremiah 29:11).

The process of working out the heavenly realities of our new birth into the earthly realm is called sanctification and it is the working of grace where we partner with God through faith. In the process, Christ's life is continually dispensed into ours as we walk with Him in sweet fellowship and obedience.

Now that you are born again, you are "in Him" and so you are automatically in the Secret Place. You have also become a member of God's big family called the Church. The Christian life is an "us life" so it is essential to belong to a church family.

If you don't belong to any local church, I will encourage you to find one that is Bible-based and Jesus focused; where the Word of God and the Spirit of God are given pre-eminence and join that family.

Though you are now totally saved and completely blessed in the realm of the spirit, it is essential to get this heavenly reality to manifest here on earth. That is where human responsibility comes into play to partner with God in the process so we can continue to maintain a conscious living and thriving relationship with God.

Like every relationship, our relationship with God needs to be nourished and nurtured so we can grow in grace and faith.

7

How to dwell in The Secret Place of the Most High

BANISH SIN-CONSCIOUSNESS

Many people run away from God because of the problem of sin. However, as a Christian, staying close to God will keep you safe from sin. God told Moses to walk before Him and be perfect. *Our perfection is significantly based on the measure of our proximity to God.* The moment you accepted Jesus as your Lord and personal saviour, you received His righteousness. You are still in the process of maturing into the nature of Christ so when your bad habits and weaknesses threaten to take over again, don't give up on yourself. Repeat loudly or quietly as many times as you need to, "I am the righteousness of God in Christ Jesus" until you believe it. Know that the enemy will never tell you anything good about yourself or your situation, so learn to identify, arrest and defeat condemning thoughts and emotions with an opposite word from God.

For instance, when you feel your former helplessness or depression returning, identify that it is the enemy trying to destroy your confidence. Respond with, for example, "Christ has been made wisdom for me, therefore I am a wise woman. I make wise decisions just like Jesus. I am improving my parenting skills as I obey the

Word of God and the counsel of the Holy Spirit for parenting each child." Or "God has not given me the spirit of fear but of power, love and sound mind. I will not give in to this panic attack, fear, and depression." Identify ungodly thoughts or desires that pop into your mind as demonic suggestions. Identify the desire for past addictions and behaviours as attacks on your faith and your relationship with God. In both cases, giving in will make you feel guilty. Dirty, and condemned, so that you will be afraid to worship and pray or even go to church. Be swift to respond by speaking the Word of God as much as you need to. Ask the Holy Spirit to help you make the right decision for that situation, and you will overcome it.

THE WORD OF GOD

In prayer, we talk to God and He talks back to us. It is easy to talk to God because we can control that, but listening to God is a challenge for many Believers because of the difficulty in discerning the voice of God from the other voices that are constantly speaking to us.

You must, therefore, learn to discern the voice of God from all the others. God speaks to His children in many ways, but to be safe, you must remain within the parameters of the Word of God: the Bible. For the believer, the Bible is God's word to you.

Rev. Kenneth Hagin emphasized this point when he stated that the Christian must see the Bible as the Word of God, that is, "God speaking to me." God will speak to you in your heart but you have to check that within the context of the Bible. If it is not in agreement with the nature and character of God, then discard that voice. The Bible is the sure Word of God. Anything you hear that is contrary to the Word of God in the Bible is not from God.

Always check what you hear from God's word and ensure it is in context and in line with the heart of God.

Jesus is The Word of God

Jesus is the word of God. John 1:1NKJV says, "in the beginning was the Word, and the Word was with God and the Word was God...and the Word became flesh and dwelt amongst us."

As we read, study, meditate on, and speak the word, we are taking Jesus into us. He commands us to abide in the Vine (John 15), and since He is the vine as well as the Word, then abiding in the Vine is abiding in the Word.

We must build a habit of reading, hearing and meditating on the Word of God. This is a sure way to success (Joshua 1:8-9). The more of Him we have through the intake of the word, the more we have to work with (more on this later).

Prayer

There is a popular children's song with the lyrics "read your Bible, pray every day … if you want to grow." As elementary and basic as this song is, it captures the basic foundation for a solid Christian life which will flourish into all the glories and treasures promised by God in His word.

Many Christians tend to neglect the important basics of the Christian life that nurtured and built them up in their faith when they began their journey. As they progress in life, many fall because they leave the important basics of their faith walk unattended.

As a seeker of God and a mother who wants to abide in the Secret Place, you must value prayer and the Word of God. A mother who will take the time to pray and to read her Bible daily is on her way to establishing a solid relationship with the God of Glory.

God is not Santa Claus

Prayer is generally perceived as talking to God and asking Him to do things for you. Though this notion of prayer is not false, it is very limited in capturing the full meaning of this awesome mystery called prayer. A better definition of prayer, in my opinion, will be *communicating with God*. This way, prayer becomes a two-way stream - a dialogue, instead of a one-way stream – a monologue. The former notion of prayer often presents God as a "Santa Claus" who exists just to give people their desires and wishes.

That is very far from the truth. God is God and He doesn't exist for our pleasure. The reverse is true – we are not God and we exist for His pleasure.

Having an audience with God is a privilege that you must greatly value. Don't take His benevolence for granted. When you approach him with an attitude of gratitude and humility, you position yourself better to receive rather than approaching him with an attitude of entitlement. He owes you nothing but you owe Him everything. He alone is God. Blessed be His holy name. Amen.

Believe and Expect an Answer

According to Mark 11:23-25, when you pray, you have to believe and expect an answer. The answer you expect may not always be something tangible; it could simply be a word from the Lord. If you don't see prayer as communication or dialogue, then you won't tune in to God to listen to Him. Jesus' prayer life was not a monologue. Every time He prayed, He expected an answer from God. You must do the same.

When you see prayer rightly as a dialogue, you will then understand that such communication can only be enriched within a thriving relationship. Yes, as a believer, you have a relationship with God but just as in the natural, relationships of all kinds require nurturing and nourishing through communication and other mutually beneficial acts of service and sacrifice, our relationship with our Heavenly Father will also have to be nurtured, nourished and developed intentionally so we can access His depths, truths and treasures *promised to those who diligently seek Him.*

Indeed, there are levels and depths in God that casual seekers can never experience. The general benevolence of God is accessible to every living being but Heaven is available to only Believers. For those who are hungry and cannot settle for the surface and survival levels, God promises to reveal His secrets to us, take us deeper into Himself to access treasures beyond measure; the secret of the Lord is with those who fear Him; moreover, no eyes have seen, no ears have heard, neither has it entered into the hearts of men the things that God has prepared for those who love Him (Psalm 25:14, 1Corinthians 2:9).

SEEK HIM DILIGENTLY

Lovers of God will seek Him diligently. Lovers of God want to stay in the Secret Place. His presence is your home and your shield.

True, God is not a respecter of persons and His benevolence is towards all men, but there are rewards and treasures reserved for diligent seekers. God's reward system is not free for all. You must qualify for it by being a diligent seeker and you will get the sure reward promised for permanent dwellers in the Secret Place (Hebrews 11:6, Psalm 91).

As we continue to grow and develop our relationship with God through the medium of prayer, we build a growing intimacy with Him which leads us straight into His heart. Heidi Baker, author of *Birthing the Miraculous,* says you are "undone" forever; that means, blessed forever. You get my point.

Prayer will transform your heart and turn you into a different person because as you talk to the Father and hear Him speak back to you, there is a spark of love and grace that transforms you from the inside and eventually shows all over you; touching every area of your life. Prayer will change you.

THE PRAYER LIFE OF JESUS CHRIST

As a permanent dweller in the Secret Place of the Most High, you have to be a person of prayer; a praying mother who is filled with the Word of God. Since Jesus is our perfect example, we must study His prayer life. Jesus taught us how to pray by using the model in Matthew 6:9-13. I will encourage you to use this model when you pray.

> [9] *"In this manner, therefore, pray:*
> *Our Father in heaven,*
> *Hallowed be Your name.*
> [10] *Your kingdom come.*
> *Your will be done*
> *On earth as it is in heaven.*
> [11] *Give us this day our daily bread.*
> [12] *And forgive us our debts,*
> *As we forgive our debtors.*
> [13] *And do not lead us into temptation,*
> *But deliver us from the evil one.*
> *For Yours is the kingdom and the power and the glory*
> *forever. Amen." (Matthew 6:9-13 NKJV)*

Looking at the model Jesus gave us, your prayer time with the Lord must include the following elements:

Honesty and Authenticity

Jesus' prayers were all heartfelt and honest. He simply expressed His heart to the Father.

For Jesus, prayer was not just a religious chore that 'He had to do'. It was a delightful and honest conversation with the Father. In John 17, Jesus talks about the love He has for the Father and how the Father loves Him and you see this holy love relationship expressed with all reverence and purity. This is romance in its purest form; *divine romance.*

The intra-Trinitarian love is the absolute beautiful love that God has for Himself – that is, the love between the Godhead (Father, Son, and Holy Spirit). Jesus always prayed from this place of love. Jesus talked with the Father honestly about everything.

At Gethsemane, Jesus, the King of Glory openly and honestly expressed His weakness as a man. Though He is God, He asked Father God to change the plan of great suffering and separation, but yet yielded to the Father's will to go to the cross.

What I like about this scene is the level of honesty and openness between Jesus and the Father. This is the example you must follow in prayer. You don't need to try to impress God with your strength or whatever you think you can offer Him. You can approach Him with all sincerity and to enable His strength and grace to flow boundlessly to you just as He did for Jesus at Gethsemane. In your time of prayer, don't be hesitant or reserved. Adopt Jesus's approach, let authenticity, honesty, and openness to the Father characterize our prayers.

Gratitude, Praise, and Worship

Prayers show gratitude and worship. Jesus was known for giving thanks to the Father when He prayed. Sometimes, that is all He said (John 11:42). In the face of an impossible task of feeding thousands of people with just a couple of fishes and bread, Jesus didn't bind and loose and command manna to fall from heaven! He only lifted the little in His hands to heaven and *gave thanks* (Luke 9:16).

In the Lord's prayer, Jesus emphasized the importance of worship when he started and ended with worship (Matthew 6:9 and 13). Jesus is King of all and approaching Him requires that you honour Him with a reverent attitude of gratitude. Before you start asking Him for things, it is important to remember what He has already done for you and give Him thanks for that first. Your life and health, and most of all the privilege of having a relationship with Him, is reason enough to give Him thanks and praise. My pastor Rev. David Antwi emphasized this point when he stated that "the reason for our worship should fundamentally be because we are blood-bought, blood-washed, and Spirit indwelt." This alone is a great reason to give God thanks and to worship Him. Be like Jesus, imitate His prayer of gratitude and worship.

Faith

"Now faith is confidence in what we hope for and assurance about what we do not see" (Hebrews 11:1 NIV).

Jesus always prayed in faith, confidence and great boldness. He never doubted the effect of His prayers. When He cursed the fig tree, He expected it to die to its roots. When He prayed for the food to multiply to feed thousands, He expected it to happen.

Jesus was never anxious that His prayers would not be answered. He had the confident assurance that what He had prayed for will happen.

He did not only pray and live by faith but He taught His disciples to do the same. In Mark 11:23 -25, Jesus taught them that when you present your desires to God, believe that you have already received it, don't doubt what you have said in prayer, and don't speak contrary to it.

In John 15, Jesus also assures us that if we abide in Him and His words abide in us, we shall ask whatever we desire and it will be given to us (John 15:7). Wow! This is so wonderful and it is true. God cannot lie! Receive and walk in this light.

Have faith in God. Believe in the faithfulness of the God you are praying to otherwise your prayer is futile. Faith is a requirement for access to God; for how can you talk with someone you don't believe exists or how can you receive from someone you don't believe has the ability to deliver?

Make the Word of God a daily priority and your faith will grow which in turn will make your prayer more effective. Spending time reading the word and listening to God helps you better understand and personalize the words in the Bible, enabling you to renew your mind and heart about various aspects of your life. When you pray after this encounter, you are able to pray from a place of boldness, which is the ingredient that makes your prayers effective.

Faith comes by hearing the Word of God (Romans 10:17). This means that faith is not something that you learn to do but something that you receive as you expose yourself to the Word of God. Faith will always come when you hear God speak. You are responsible for proactively setting yourself up to hear the Word of God regularly so you can build your faith.

Early morning prayers: Starting the day with Prayer

There is something about morning prayers. I think it is to do with the principle of first things. Recognizing our need for God should compel us to seek Him first before we attend to other things.

Jesus always rose early in the morning whilst it was still dark to go into a secluded place to pray (Mark 1:35). He had a culture of praying early in the morning.

Putting God first will set you up for greater success.

Quality Time in His Presence

Jesus had a culture of spending quality time in prayer. Jesus would rise early in the morning to spend quality time with God. He also prayed all night before choosing His disciples (Luke 6:12). Sometimes, it is essential to prevail in prayer till we have "prayed through."

Prayer is not an empty religious activity but a real spiritual exercise and you must be willing to invest the necessary time needed to ensure you breakthrough in prayer. Every victory you want to see in the physical realm has to be won in the spiritual realm first because the spiritual precedes the physical. You win in the spirit through prayer.

Persistence is often the price required to ensure your prayers reach the dimensions needed to secure certain levels of victory. Jesus emphasized the principle of persistence in prayer in the parable in Luke 18:1-7. Here, He stated that men always ought to pray and not faint.

Like the persistent woman who will not give the unrighteous judge rest till he gave her justice, we must also continue to prevail and push in prayer against all odds:

> "Then He spoke a parable to them, that men always ought to pray and not lose heart, ² saying: "There was in a certain city a judge who did not fear God nor regard man. ³ Now there was a widow in that city; and she came to him, saying,²'Get justice for me from my adversary. ⁴And he would not for a while; but afterward he said within himself, 'Though I do not fear God nor regard man, ⁵ yet because this widow troubles me I will avenge her, lest by her continual coming she weary me.'"⁶Then the Lord said, "Hear what the unjust judge said. ⁷And shall God not avenge His own elect who cry out day and night to Him, though He bears long with them?" (Luke 18:1-7 NKJV)

In my personal experience in prayer, I have come to realise that God always has things He wants to show and teach us. There are secrets He wants to reveal to us. To receive all this goodness requires quality time in His presence. These moments are precious and should not be rushed. We must be willing to wait and stay as long as is required to see the breakthrough needed in prayer. In the charismatic world, we call this "prevailing prayer" or "praying through." Receiving from God demands a calm mind resting and trusting in Him. This could mean staying longer in His presence.

Making the time to just listen and receive from God is time well spent. When you are not in a rush, you can receive more from your Lord through studying the Word, meditating on the word, or simply soaking in His presence with some great worship music. Prayer is a conversation, so don't just come with a list of requests and complaints and rush off. Give God the opportunity to speak, too.

Time with God is a delight when we do it the right way; nothing is boring about it. I always leave His presence wanting more of Him and feeling that I have not finished with Him. One day I asked God in prayer about this and He said it is a good sign; hunger for more of God is a sign that you are alive unto Him. He is so good you just can't have enough of Him.

Though it is not always easy waking up early to pray, you can implement strategies to help you. Start with what you can reasonably manage and ask God to help you. As you begin, He will continue to draw you to Himself and all too soon, it will become a habit!

Desire

Desire is an essential element to achieving great and impossible things. When you strongly desire something, it is just a matter of time and that thing will be drawn to you. If you strongly desire something, no price is too high for you to pay to obtain it. You develop desire through exposure.

When you expose yourself to something long enough, you begin to desire it. As a Christian, you have the Holy Spirit in you and He is working in you both to will (desire) and to do His good pleasure which includes spending time with God. Hence, developing desire for more of God comes easy when you turn your heart towards Him by exposing yourself to His word, fellowshipping with other Believers, and giving attention to spiritual exercises such as fasting.

As your desire for Him increases, passion will begin to build up and dwelling in the Secret Place becomes natural for you because you just can't have enough of Him.

During prayer, ask God to continually draw you to Himself. Jesus emphasized that unless the Father draws you, you can't come to Him (John 6:44); by implication, the quest for more of God in you is always initiated by God.

Acknowledge Him as the source of your passion and remain hooked to Him knowing that without Him you can do nothing (John 15:5). It is He who is working in you to will and to do His good pleasure. He who has begun a good work of sparking the desire for Himself in you will also be faithful to keep you going and drawing you even deeper and deeper into Himself till you are overshadowed and constituted with Himself.

Don't stop until you are conformed to the perfect image of His Glorious Son. Hold on to His hands by faith and walk this journey with Him. He is faithful to keep you. Don't stop desiring. Keep pushing and He will pull you up (James 4:8).

Jesus Practiced the Presence of God

The final thing I will say about Jesus' prayer life is that He lived in constant awareness of God's presence and was always in tune with heaven. His heartbeat was in rhythm with the flow of heaven.

He lived out the scripture that urges us to pray without ceasing (1 Thessalonians 5:17) or to put it differently, He practised the presence of God continually.

Jesus was always aware of God's presence with Him and was in communication with the Father and in tune with Him all the time. Whatever was going on in Heaven was so real to Jesus that He simply duplicated that on earth (John 5:19). It is no wonder He taught His disciples to pray, "Thy will be done on earth as it is in heaven" (Matthew 6:10). Jesus lived "heaven on earth."

Ephesians 5:1 tells us to imitate God as beloved children. You must imitate the earth-life of Jesus. You may think that such a standard is just too high for you to aspire to, but you can do it by His grace. Living in the consciousness of His presence will enable you to pray unceasingly. Just like Jesus, you will know that you are never alone because you abide/live/remain in the presence of God, in the Secret Place of the Most High.

These truths about Jesus' prayer life inform us that prayer is "a vital necessity for daily survival" as the Archbishop Nicholas Duncan Williams rightly stated. I believe in prayer. I believe a prayerless Christian is so vulnerable to satanic attacks and would not attain the best God has for him. According to Apostle Paul, "all things are yours" (1 Corinthians 3:21), but you can't access heavenly realities and riches without a strong living connection to God through the mystery medium of prayer.

As a mother who wants to dwell in the Secret Place, determine to learn from Jesus and build a daily prayer altar where you will meet with God and spend quality time talking with Him before you start your day.

I will now share a couple of practical tips that will help you build a thriving and exciting consistent prayer life.

How to Build a Thriving Prayer Life

Ask God to help you

To build a habit of daily prayer is not an easy task. True prayer that moves heaven is a spiritual exercise which threatens the kingdom of darkness. Because it is so vital for connection with God, Satan will fight it.

A mother who will succeed at maintaining a strong, consistent, and thriving prayer life will have to start with God's help.

Begin your journey of prayer by honestly expressing to God your sincere desire to build a strong prayer life.

Ask Him to help you start each day with a conversation with Him. God's word promises us that if we ask, we will receive (John

16:24). So just ask Him to help you wake up earlier so you can spend time with Him. Remember that the desire to seek God and to spend time with Him is initiated by God Himself, "for it is God who works in you both to will and to do for *His* good pleasure" (Philippians 2:13)

Asking for God's help to pray is in His absolute will. God will answer you and He will help you. I am a living witness of this truth. It is He who is my strength, I know for a fact that without Him I can do nothing (John 15:5)!

Ask Him to help you and it will amaze you what God will do through you as you get into deep fellowship with Him in prayer. God is faithful. He will surely give you the grace you need to wake you and pray.

Walking with God is a partnership which can only work with your active responsibility. When you ask God to help you, He will supply the grace and help needed to pray, but you will have to reach out in faith to take it. For example, when you ask God to wake you up early to pray and your eyes pop open at 4am, don't toss around and say, "it is too early, let me catch an extra 30 minutes of sleep." No! Don't do that! Take advantage of the grace and jump out of bed and head straight to your prayer closet! You can do this in the mighty name of Jesus.

Set your alarm to wake up early

As mentioned above, God works in partnership with us. My pastor, Rev. David Antwi, has often said that, "the faith that makes God absolutely responsible is an irresponsible faith." I agree. God does not control us like robots. We are co-labourers with Him and we must put all our effort into our relationship with Him. God works with us.

With this understanding, it is important to put some practical measures in place that will help you achieve this important goal of establishing a habit of daily prayer.

One of such is setting your alarm to wake up earlier than usual. Start with a time that you can manage. Work with your faith at the level you are at. The Christian walk is a journey of grace and faith and we grow in it so don't overwhelm yourself.

For instance, if you have been praying for 5 minutes and you want to do more, don't set your alarm to wake up 30 minutes earlier. Start small.

You can add an extra 2 minutes, then you go to 5, then at a point, you can manage 20 minutes or 30 or even an hour. Just start from where you are and stay consistent and you will see growth.

After you set your alarm ask God to help you wake up. When you combine faith and a strong determination, nothing can stop you. Indeed there is nothing like a made-up mind backed by strong faith! You can do this.

Wake up!

In order to fulfil any goal, it is important to match it with the necessary disciplines required to accomplish the accompanying daily activities. If you are going to establish and maintain a habit of prayer, then you will need the discipline to stick with your daily prayer routine.

Believe that as a faithful Father, God will always do His part to help you when you ask Him to. He is too faithful and will not flout His word - when you pray for help, He will answer you (Jeremiah 33:3). However, God will not do your part for you. Therefore, when your alarm goes off wake up! That is your responsibility and you can do it.

Take steps to ensure you are well awake and don't fall back asleep; especially, during the very early hours when other members of your family are still snoozing. To avoid the temptation of snuggling under the covers again, you can brush your teeth and wash your face or take a shower, or have a cup of coffee. Whatever works for you, go for it and make sure you are awake. It is worth it.

When I was at secondary school in Ghana, some students tried various crazy tricks to keep themselves awake in order to study longer during exams week. Some drank dark coffee, others woke up at dawn, showered and dressed up to help them stay awake and others did other strange things - like soaking their feet in a bucket of cold water - just to ensure they stayed awake to study. Though some of these examples may sound extreme, they demonstrate the efforts made by determined students who placed a high level of importance on passing their exams.

How much value do you place on your prayer life? What are you willing to sacrifice to ensure you establish an uncompromising prayer life? Think about it. If you value your time with God, you will make the effort and take every necessary step to ensure you pray every day.

Create a favourable atmosphere for prayer

Prayer is all about fellowship and relationship and thus, the atmosphere you create can enhance or hinder the flow of your time with the Lord.

You can begin your prayer time with some good worship music that will help you focus on God. Like the Psalmist admonishes us in Psalm 100:4, you are to enter His gates with thanksgiving and His courts with praise, then arrive in His presence with worship and adoration.

Singing has a way of inviting God's presence in a strong way. The Bible commands us to come before His presence with singing (Psalm 100:2). Get into the mood with great worship. However, you don't have to know how to sing to do this. Just connect your heart with the worship music you are playing, sing-along, hum, or just flow in the spirit.

This is what I normally do and it really helps me get into the flow. You can adopt it too or choose what works best for you. The most important thing is that you connect your heart with God and not just pass time. Following the protocol of entering His presence through thanksgiving, praise, and worship is the way prescribed by scripture and it always works (Psalm 100:4, Matthew 6:9).

Praying in the spirit is also a wonderful way of "getting into the spirit". When you pray in the spirit you are actually strengthening your spirit man or as the Bible puts it "edifying" yourself. You tap into the rhythm of God's heart quicker when you pray in the spirit. The problem of "praying amiss" would be avoided because you don't pray against God's will when you pray in the spirit.

If you don't pray in the sprit (called "praying in tongues"), this will be a great time for you to ask the Father to give you this awesome gift of the Holy Spirit by baptizing you in the Holy Ghost.

Enter into conversation with God

The model prayer Jesus taught His disciples is the safest way to pray so you don't pray amiss. Follow the format of the Lord's Prayer and stay within the parameters of God's will in prayer.

Don't be religious or rigid when it comes to prayer. Prayer is a conversation in a love relationship and so you really can't stick to a formula.

There are no rigid rules in love!

Use the model as a standard in your daily prayer routine but flow with what is really on your heart. This makes your prayer authentic and genuine. God is not impressed with phoney and religious acts that are not heart-borne. Jesus was not impressed with the Pharisees and Sadducees because all their religious acts and rigid standards where merely outward without a heart connection.

Insisting on sticking to rules when it comes to conversation with God will put you in the same class of hypocrites as the Pharisees unless you connect your heart to what you are doing.

In Gethsemane, Jesus didn't follow a format; He just poured out His heart to the Father. God responds to honest hearts. Learn to enter into honest conversation with God with no religious words such as "thee" and "thou"! Though they may sound holy, they really mean nothing unless they are spoken from a sincere and genuine heart.

Be yourself and open up to the Father. It will amaze you how His love and grace will flow to you as you relate with Him in authenticity and openness.

Always remember this: prayer is a love relationship and there are no formulas with love.

Seek God, not an experience

Hebrews 11:6 says that God rewards those who seek Him diligently. There are many scriptures that emphasise the importance God places on His children seeking Him, not just seeking the things He can give them.

There are many scriptures that command us to seek His face, not to forsake the Lord, or draw near to God, and others telling us that God is interested in having a genuine relationship with us (Psalm 27:8, Jeremiah 29:13, James 4:8). God is more interested in this relationship than just being our provider. In fact, Matthew 6:33 tells us to seek first the Kingdom of God and then all other things will be added to us. The Kingdom of God is about God and His agenda.

Unfortunately, many Christians have limited prayer to just asking God to do things for them. Many of our prayer lists are choked with demands for things, "God give me this, and give me that now!"

Though we are allowed and encouraged to ask for things in prayer, that is not the core nor the main focus of prayer. I strongly believe the focus of our prayers must be God Himself. He does care about our needs and urges us not to worry but to cast all our cares upon Him and He will take care of us. However, if we limit prayer to only asking for things, then it becomes a one-way stream; a very unhealthy and unbalanced relationship.

Do you care about how God feels? Is He on the other end

simply to receive your problems and 'throw' down blessings to you? Obviously, that is not right.

All healthy relationships must be mutually beneficial. We must care about each other and the focus should not be on what we can get from each other but rather on nurturing the relationship in genuine love and caring about each other's needs and desires. Love gives. We give Him our adoration and our lives. He is worthy of it all.

To nurture this divine relationship, makes time to just to sit with Jesus and love on Him. Just enjoy His company and let Him know that He is enough for you. Don't use God for your personal gain! It is not fair!

The Lord loves it when we just come to Him with no agenda but just to be with Him. This is true love and prayer is best enjoyed when we take this approach. We connect with His heart and He gives us His heartbeat for His purposes which we can then carry to fulfil His will on earth.

You may ask, "how do I just go to God with no agenda when I have so many needs?" By all means, cast your cares upon Him, trusting Him to take care of you. Honestly, sometimes, our problems can be so overwhelming that they overshadow everything else on our mind. In a situation like that, don't pretend before God and act as if it doesn't matter.

Rather, pour out your heart to Him and give Him the burden, then get into worship, acknowledging His power to save. This is what Jesus did at Gethsemane. Honesty and sincerity are the keys to great intimacy but remember to acknowledge God as all-powerful and worship Him simply for who He is.

Listen to God

According to Psalm 29:4, the voice of the Lord is powerful and majestic. Jesus also declared in John 6:63 that "...The words that I speak to you are spirit, and *they* are life". Never miss out on what

God has to say to you when you go into prayer. The voice of the Lord will transform your life.

Don't spend all your prayer time talking to God without carving sufficient time to intentionally listen to Him. You listen by being quiet before Him and asking Him to speak to you both in your heart and through His word, as you study the scriptures.

When you are waiting to hear Him speak, you can either turn everything off so you can be attentive to His voice or you can play some calm worship instrumental music.

Ensure your focus is on Jesus by either reading or meditating on scripture. Never blank your mind as other religions do. Focus on God's word and expect to hear from Him.

Always have a journal so you can document what God says to you in your heart or the revelations He gives you from His word.

God does speak in diverse ways that are biblically authentic. These include visions, dreams, inner witness, impressions, and even audibly. After you have heard from God, it is important that you always check the authenticity of the message from scripture – the spirit of the word, not just the letter. This means it must be in context and flow with the Spirit of Christ (Isaiah 8:20, Psalm 119:30, Hebrews 4:12). Remember even the devil quoted scriptures to Jesus when he tempted Him, but he did it out of context and with the wrong spirit (Matthew 4:6).

You check what you hear by finding out what the Bible says about it, and the context in which it was said. Also, check your spirit to find out if you have peace about the word you have received. This is because as a Christian, the Spirit of God will bear witness in your own spirit about everything. Deep inside, you will know all things because the Spirit will teach you and lead you into all truth. (John 14:26, Romans 8:16, Proverbs 20:27)

Be careful not to believe every voice you hear but check everything from scripture (1 John 4:1). The Bible, the testimony of Jesus Christ, is the true word and voice of God (2 Peter 1:19). God will never say something to you that contradicts His word, His nature, and His ways.

You are always safe in the Word of God.

These are just a few things that I have learnt about prayer and I hope it helps you. I know there is so much more to learn about the mystery of prayer and every day as we make time to seek God, He will continually draw us ever closer to Himself. As you continue to develop your prayer life, spending time with God becomes a delight and you just can't wait to meet with Him in the mornings.

8

DAILY ROUTINE IN THE SECRET PLACE

Dwelling implies doing life with Jesus. Your fellowship with the Lord should not end when your morning prayer ends. Since you dwell in the Secret Place, you must remain there even when you leave home for work, school, shopping or any other activity that is scheduled for the day.

Throughout your day, you should stay connected with the Lord. He's got to be involved in every detail of your life.

Jesus should be Lord over *all* aspects of your life; not just quiet time or Sundays. He must reign in everything we think, say and do.

Throughout the Bible, God reveals His desire to keep company with His people. Many have missed out on this because they maintain the legalism of religion. God is not as interested in the things we do and the rituals that accompany them as He is in our true intimate fellowship with Him. The concept of the House of God or the Church is evidence of God's purpose to have an intimate relationship with His people. His ultimate desire and purpose are to dwell amongst His people. He is not a distant God (Revelations 21:3)[2].

In Exodus 24, God instructed the people of Israel not to come near Him because of His absolute Holiness that cannot tolerate sin.

---

[2] Also see Rev. David Antwi's message on the House of God at Kharis.org

However, in verse 10, the Bible states that Moses and the leaders actually went up and saw the Lord and even described the glorious features around His feet but they didn't die. I had to go back and listen to that passage of the audio Bible again because it sounded contradictory to what God had said earlier. I believe that it shows how God's graciousness supersedes His rules (Exodus 24:1-10).

God's initial plan for His people was for all to be priests and kings unto Him but due to sin, only Aaron and his sons were given this privilege (Exodus 19:6). In Christ, however, God restores His original plan of having a kingdom of royal priests and a holy people set apart for His glory. He "has made us kings and priests unto God and his Father; to him be glory and dominion forever and ever. Amen" (Revelations 1:6 NKJV). Again, the Apostle Paul reminds us, "But you *are* a chosen generation, a royal priesthood, a holy nation, His special people, that you may proclaim the praises of Him who called you out of darkness into His marvellous light" (1Peter 2:9 NKJV).

God is calling us into a daily walk of sweet fellowship with Him. As a caring Father who made us for His glory, He doesn't want us to miss out on the privileges of living our daily lives with Him. We are honoured to have access to the Lord of Lords who is happy to do life with us to the very minute detail, even in the mundane activities of life.

Oh, what a privilege it is to walk with Jesus every minute of the day.

Isaiah 26:3 tells us we will enjoy peace if we maintain a vital connection with God by keeping our minds stayed on Him and Joshua 1:8-9 God prescribes His word on our lips and in our hearts/minds constantly as the means to a successful life.

In the New Testament, the Apostle Paul revealed that the secret to transformation or a changed life is the result of changing how you think (Romans 12:2).

The life Christ promises us is glorious but it can only be experienced practically by those who make the Lord their dwelling place – those who are in Him not just in theory but for real. Indeed, those who choose to live every day with Jesus in obedience will see His glory.

Now, Let's get practical here! How do we constantly engage God in everything when we don't see Him physically? I'm glad you asked this question because it can be frustrating when you know you have to do something but just don't know how to do it.

I have taken the time to research on this subject and I have discovered some practical tools given to us in scripture that can help us develop a lifestyle that involves and engages God beyond the church premises into everyday practical living.

The object is to ensure we walk in continual consciousness of His presence and maintain a continual conversation with Him as a constant present Friend. This is popularly called "the practice of His presence" or according to Dr Caroline Leaf, an established continual "internal dialogue" with God. For a person doing this, God is never far away; such a one is a dweller in the Secret Place and the Lord is her habitation.

Now, let's look at these tools in detail and how to practically employ them in our daily living. I can confidently say that these truths have helped me maintain the discipline and bliss of walking with Jesus in everyday living. I believe they will help you too.

BIBLICAL MEDITATION

In recent years, meditation has become very popular especially with the surge of the New Age Religion and emphasis on humanism and self-power. The type of meditation exercised by the world is however, very different from what the Bible commands us to do.

The Christian meditation is not emptying the mind as practised by the world but actually "filling the mind," with God's word as stated by Bill Johnson in his book "The War in Your Head".

Meditation is thinking on the Word of God, brooding over it through the day, asking questions about it in your mind, talking to God about it and asking for more revelation on that particular subject.

Bill Johnson stated in his book, *The War in Your Head*, that worrying is a negative kind of meditation. If you can flip it around and use the same method and apply it to the Word of God, then you will be skilled at meditating.

BIBLICAL MEDITATION REQUIRES INTENTIONALITY AND DISCIPLINE

We must take meditation seriously because it is one of the main ways that we can transform our lives by renewing our minds (Romans 12:2). Before becoming Believers, we were separated from God and our thoughts, values, and ideals were opposite to the ways of God which consequently produced a depraved lifestyle (Ephesians 4:17-19). When we get born again, although our spirit gets saved and perfect, our minds and flesh don't change automatically.

God gives us the responsibility of undergoing the change through the help of His spirit in addition to other spiritual tools which He has made available to us such us the Word of God, prayer, and meditation.

MONITOR YOUR THOUGHTS

Scripture commands us to bring every thought captive to the obedience of Christ. Obeying this instruction requires strong mental discipline that can only be attained if we are in tune with our thoughts and can decipher which thought is from God and which ones we need to cast down. Meditation on the Word of God will help establish God's truth in your mind so you can discern correctly truth from lies.

Dr Caroline Leaf, bestselling author of *The Perfect You* suggests that if we are to bring every thought captive as the Bible commands us to do, then according to scientific research, that means we are supposed to talk with God every 10 seconds. Meditating on God's word will help us immensely in establishing this important internal dialogue with God.

God wants us to be transformed to become just like Jesus but transformation can only happen when we change the way we think through reading, hearing and meditating on the Word of God (Romans 12:2, Joshua 1:8-9, 2 Corinthians 3:18).

In Proverbs 23:7, the Bible makes it clear that our thoughts define us, "For as he thinks in his heart, so *is* he." Dr. Cindi Trimm, in her book *Hello Tomorrow* stated that "your feet can never take you where your mind has not been." In other words, every physical change must of necessity be preceded by a mental change.

Occasionally, accidents or divine interventions may cause a change but that is not the norm. Even when changes occur without your disciplined effort, it must be maintained by changing your mindset to conform to the new you.

In Joshua 1:8-9, God instructed Joshua to take His word seriously and meditate on it day and night to attain success. Meditation is huge for every successful living. It is quite a shame that Christians have neglected this precious tool given to us by God Himself. Well, we take it back in Jesus name! Amen!

I think this is enough to understand that we cannot do life with Jesus unless we engage Him in our minds through scriptural meditation.

I have observed that many people in the Christian world have been silent on the subject of meditation, probably because it requires discipline that seems to be lacking in the modern-day church. Nevertheless, we can't skip it if we are to become all that God wants us to be. Indeed, if God has commanded it, then we can do it. Joshua did it, the Apostle Paul did it, and in recent times, many are discovering this truth and applying it to their lives with great success. You and I can also do it in Jesus's mighty name! Amen!

The art of Biblical meditation is surely a great way to stay connected with God. It is simply setting the Lord before you always as David did (Psalm 16:8).

Be like the psalmist who said, "But as for me, the nearness of God is my good; I have made the Lord GOD my refuge, That I may tell of all Your work." (Psalm 73:28 NASB – New American Standard Bible). Developing a daily habit of meditating on the Bible will keep us constantly in tune with God as dwellers in the Secret Place.

Bring your thoughts captive with the Word of God

A believer respects and acts on God's word (Isaiah 43:26, Matthew 24:35). Knowing and praying the Word of God brings results. When you know what God has said about each situation and you meditate on the relevant Bible verses, your faith will grow immensely, making it easier to receive these promises of God that you are convinced about.

You can make a list of God's promises for every situation you are facing and soak in them through meditation. Once it is settled in your heart, begin to confess them and they will become your possession (Mark 11:23 – 25).

I have personally become more active in meditating on God's word and I am seeing a great change in my life. The Bible emphasizes greatly on the importance of managing our thoughts and bringing *every thought* captive to the obedience of Christ. We simply can't allow your thoughts to just go in any direction, we must take charge of every thought and conform it to God's word.

According to Dr Caroline Leaf, "thoughts are real physical things that occupy mental real estate." Our thoughts shape us just us Proverbs 23:7 confirms.

The state of our thoughts and mind is what determines the outcome of our lives. Ephesians 4 and 5 clearly shows us that the ungodly and worldly are depraved because the *"futility of their mind, having their understanding darkened, being alienated from the life of God"* (Ephesians 4:17 NKJV). The born-again believer is however admonished to separate themselves from the above by making a switch in their minds; we are admonished to be renewed in the spirit of our minds or as Paul puts it again in Romans 12:2, we are to renew our minds to be transformed.

Mind work is so much important than the merit it has received in the modern church.

We are of course not to seek mental excellence at the expense of building up our spirit but the needed importance has to be given to every aspect of our being: Spirit, Soul, and Body. The Word of God must touch our spirit, soul, and body.

One person who heeded to the instruction of God to keep His mind on God and to speak His word is Joshua – like his mentor Moses who will not go anywhere without God's presence, Joshua obeyed God to the core and he had tremendous success with no defeat except for the issue with Ai which was rectified when he promptly obeyed God.

As we behold Him, we become like Him.

Romans 12:1-2 shows us that change/transformation is only possible when we renew our minds. That means change begins when we change the way we think. My pastor emphasized this truth when he said: "the gateway to the spirit is your mind." This is powerful. We access the spirit realm with our thoughts.

Don't just allow thoughts to be popping in and out of your mind. You must obey God's command to bring *every* thought captive to the obedience of Christ. You must be careful about what you are thinking and make it work for you and not against you because your life will be filled with the things you think about. Words and thoughts are related – for out of the abundance of the heart the mouth speaks and out of the abundance of the heart flows the issues of your life (Matthew 12:34, Proverbs 4:23). This is so deep. Meditating on God's word is crucial for your life if you are ever to manifest as the son of God.

A great example of meditation and manifestation is Abraham and Sarah. I know they meditated because you can't continue to say something if that is not what you are meditating on. In their naturally hopeless situation, they did not conform to the world's opinion and standards but rather switched and decided to obey what God had said. They took His word to heart, thought on it and then spoke it until they saw it happen in their lives (Genesis 17:5, Genesis 18:12-14, Genesis 21:1).

They presented their frail bodies to God as a living sacrifice, enduring the mockery of the world as they spoke and declared that they were the mother and father of many nations – in the process they were transformed from their impossible physical realities into the manifestation of the promises of God. Glory to God!

When you choose to believe and obey God, meditating and speaking His word, you open up to the supernatural realities of His word to find expression in your life. Praise God!

THE METHOD OF CHRISTIAN MEDITATION

Let me repeat that Christian meditation is not like yoga and other types of meditation which require emptying the mind; rather, it requires filling the mind with God's truth – His Word. Meditating on God's Word starts by saturating your heart and mind with God's Word. This means that you need to develop a habit of reading and hearing God's Word. Start with a daily quiet time when you study the scriptures. You can then build a habit of listening to the Bible, good preaching messages, and even some God-inspired worship music to help you create "a Word-filled atmosphere" as my pastor puts it. From the rich resource of God's Word, you have through the habit of reading and hearing, you can now proceed to practical daily mediation.

PICK A SCRIPTURE TO FOCUS ON FOR THE DAY

Every day, take one scripture to meditate on.

This doesn't have to be a long passage. It can be a verse or even a single word. Normally this could be one that jumps up to you in your study or as you listen to a message, or it could be a scripture that concerns with an issue you are dealing with.

It does not mean that you always have to wait till you feel or sense something before you choose a word to meditate on.

It is good to move with conviction so when you feel strongly about a word or phrase, it may be the Lord drawing your attention to that word or phrase, so pay attention and meditate on it so you can get more understanding and revelation on it.

If you feel or sense nothing, it doesn't mean that you can't choose a word for meditation. Decide on a subject that you may currently be studying or a word that is relevant to your current circumstance or situation. For instance, if you are dealing with an issue of sickness, meditating on a scripture that promises God's healing will be of great help to you.

LINE UPON LINE, PRECEPT UPON PRECEPT

Do not rush when you are meditating on the word.

The word is loaded with virtue so it is good to take your time to chew on it. You can take it one word at a time. Every word and its meaning matter. You get a lot from scripture when you meditate like that.

KEEP THE WORD BEFORE YOU

The art of meditation must be intentional and very proactive. The psalmist said, "I have set the Lord before me always because he is at my right hand, I shall not be moved" (Psalm 16:8). How did the Psalmist set the Lord before him? He couldn't have placed God like a picture frame before his sight.

I believe, he was talking about a deliberate effort in ensuring that he did everything possible to keep the Lord on his mind all the time. It connotes effort and intentionality.

People 'set the Lord before them' by placing tokens insight that reminds them of God or prompts them to read and meditate on the word. I write down a scripture in the morning both on my phone and on a post-it so I can look at it and meditate on it as I go about my day. Taking out some quality time to meditate is great. But the aim is to maintain a continual internal dialogue with God so the communication must continue even after having the quality time of meditation.

The way that I find to be effective for regular mediation is taking a minute every so often to think on the word. I often close my eyes for a minute and think about the word. I ask God questions and relate the word to any situation or worry on my mind. Amazing revelations flow as I do this. In Bill Johnson's book, *Way of Life*, Bill stated that he would often take a one-minute break every so often and turn his affections towards God in adoration. I think this is sweet and delightsome to God.

These are just a few of the ways you can meditate on God's word. You can choose one that works for you and make it a habit. You will be glad you did.

LIFE APPLICATION

During meditation, think about how to apply the word to your life. How does the scripture apply to you as an individual? What is your responsibility in making it happen? Is it all about God or do you have a part to play? What changes are you required to make? Do you need a divine strategy to make it happen?

Do you have the required faith to get it done? Can you do this or receive this? Be honest and sincere about your thoughts about the scripture you are meditating on and you will find God opening your eyes to truths that will transform not just you but all around you.

EXAMINE YOUR HEART

When I meditate on God's word, I often find it important to examine myself to see if there are any areas that I need to make a change to see the promises of God manifest in my life.

Meditation brings clarity. Take the opportunity during meditation to examine yourself - see if there are any obstacles to the manifestation of God's promises in your life, what to repent from, what changes need to be made, and what adjustments are required.

In meditation ask yourself these questions and answer them:

- What are the obstacles to applying or receiving the blessing in that scripture?
- Am I perfectly aligned with the Word of God?
- Am I opposing God in the area I am meditating on?
- Is my lifestyle in agreement with the conditions required for the particular promise or word?
- What do I have to do?
- Do I need help to do this?
- Honestly examine yourself and ask if this is true, how come it is not happening in your life?
- What must I change to see this promise?

As you do this, the Spirit of God will flood your soul with His light and give you great illumination. You will find that other scriptures are connected and He will lead you into all truth as He promised (John 16:13).

I strongly encourage you to actively build the habit of meditating on God's word. This simple act of obedience will open up the treasures of heaven to you like nothing else.

In Matthew 13, After Jesus taught the multitude in parables, His disciples went to Him in private and asked why He taught in parables. His answer was surprising to me as I meditated on that scripture.

Jesus said, "to you, it has been given to know the mysteries of the Kingdom but to them, it has not been given" (Matthew 13:11 NKJV). This informs us about the benefits for those who decide to dig a little deeper. Here are some of the points I got from meditating on this.

- The Kingdom's treasures are available through the Word of God.
- These treasures are a mystery; that means they are like covered truths – they are not straight forward.
- God has chosen to give some people access to these mysteries but this privilege is not available to all.
- It is the prerogative of God and we cannot question Him about that because He is God – the All-Wise God. It is a privilege to be given access into His mysteries as a disciple.
- You as a Christian have access to understand the mysteries of God.

The other thing I discovered from this scripture is even more wonderful. After Jesus told the disciples that it has been given to them to know God's mysteries, understanding of that particular parable didn't come to them automatically; they had to *ask* Him for the meaning. This is huge. *Having access doesn't mean having possession.*

You have to utilize your access by asking, seeking, and knocking. It is the glory of Kings to hide a matter but it is the glory of kings to search it out (Proverbs 25:2). We have been given the privilege and responsibility of digging deep through prayer, study, and meditation for the mysteries of the gospel to be revealed to us.

This implies that those who just hear the word once and forget about it without meditating on it or studying it further, will not discover the treasures therein and hence cannot bear fruit from that word.

Meditation is a blessing. For all who want to experience God for real, meditation cannot be ignored.

God's will for us is that we prosper and be in health even as our souls prosper. As we heed to His instruction in Joshua 1:8-9, success shall be ours.

A NOTE OF CAUTION

Please note that I am not asking you to neglect your work and other relationships as you spend time meditating on God's word throughout the day. No, that is not right. God is a God of excellence and meditation doesn't have to interfere with your work and other aspects of your daily routine.

I stated earlier on that you are meant to do life with God. That means that you do your work with Him. Don't neglect the work whilst meditating but engage God in the work by applying the word to the physical task at hand.

Meditation will enable you to improve your work until you become excellent even in the things your formerly found difficult because God is so excellent that when you have Him on your mind, you simply can't be mediocre, dishonest, or unsuccessful. Your relationships will be enriched because God is love and having Him close through meditation will ensure you never miss an opportunity to show love and care.

There are many things working against your pursuit of God so you have to be intentionally diligent and militant about keeping your mind stayed on God. His grace is sufficient for you as you keep on pursuing Him. He will help you. Meditation will certainly give you success.

Secondly, to stay safe in this practice, make sure your conversations with God are biblically based. By this I mean, for example, you wouldn't go and take something that is not yours because you were talking to God and God said to do that. That will be absurd. It is very important to be honest in your conversations with God but ensure that whatever information you are receiving back is based on scripture. Stay within the context of the scriptures and you will be safe.

SOME KEY AREAS FOR MEDITATION

Although you can choose what scriptures to meditate on, there are some key truths in scriptures that need to be ingrained on your heart and mind. These truths are basic to who we are in Christ and I believe focusing on them in meditation will do us good. Here are some of these truths.

THE LOVE OF GOD

The Bible says God's love is better than life (Psalm 63:3). As Believers in Christ, we are eternally loved with the same love that God loves Jesus with. This is huge but do you believe it? When you grasp the amazing love of God, you will be transformed and so will your world. You must focus on this love until you have believed it fully to the point that nothing can separate you from God's love (Romans 8.35-39).

Walking in the love of God starts with becoming 'God loves me' minded. As a child of God, Jesus commands you to love just as He loves. You can't give out His love if you are not convinced about it yourself. The more you accept this love the more loving you can be and the more conscious you will be of Him because God is love.

It is worth taking time to soak in the love of God by meditating on scriptures that tell you God loves you. I will encourage you to stay on these scriptures until you are absorbed into His love that nothing can ever make you doubt His love. Some of the Scriptures on God's love include the following:

> *"What manner of love the Father has bestowed on us,*
> *that we should be called children of God! Therefore,*

*the world does not know us, because it did not know
Him"* 1 John 3:1 NKJV

*"And we have known and believed the love that God
has for us. God is love, and he who abides in love
abides in God, and God in him"* 1 John 4:16 NKJV

*"Greater love has no one than this than to lay down
one's life for his friends."* John 15:13 NKJV

I will encourage you to meditate on the love of God until it
settles so deep in you. This will immerse you deeply into God and
fear will flee from you because perfect love casts out fear (1 John
4:18).

THE IMPACT OF THE LOVE OF GOD

One of the strongest bonds that will keep you glued to the
Secret Place is the bond of love; the love of God. During difficult
times, the enemy will ensure that he makes things appear worse to
you by bombarding your mind with thoughts of failure and guilt.
One of the main ways to overcome this is by being confident in the
unfailing love of God.

A good revelation of the unfailing love of God will keep you
anchored in His presence continually. Many people often tend to
run away from God when times get hard or most often when they
'fail God'. This is a very dangerous approach to take because running
from God is inevitably running into the arms of the wicked one and
you don't want to do that.

God's love for His children is a covenant love that is not based on
our performance. Ephesians 2:4 - 7 talks about how God extended
His rich mercies to us when we were dead in our sins and controlled
by lusts and wrath. He saved us not because we deserved it nor
earned it by our good works.

He did it out of the riches of His mercies and the great love He has for us. Just as we didn't earn this by our performance, nothing we can do or not do will ever make Him love us less.

The way we get saved (by grace alone through faith), is the same way we stay saved. This is very hard on the flesh because we always want to do something to earn something by our performance. When it comes to the love of God, performance doesn't earn anything. Our righteousness is as filthy rags before Him.

Being convinced of the absolute non-judgmental love of God, Jesus was able to run to the Father to dare ask Him to "take this cup" from Him. Such a daring conversation can only take place in a very safe, trusting and loving relationship where you know your vulnerability will never be used against you.

We have the same relationship with God just as Jesus does and yes, we can and must be "brutally honest" before the Lord as Kenneth Copeland rightly puts it.

Knowing and flowing in the love of God is the fuel for your continual spiritual walk. Without the conviction and settled knowledge and acceptance of the love of God, practising His presence will be impossible. For how can you be convinced that God is with you if you are not certain about His love for you regardless of your imperfections.

The love of God will keep you going when you feel incapable, low and unable to carry on. His love sustains and carries you through the toughest of seasons. Without absorbing the love of God, the inevitable pitfalls and failures in the journey can stop you, but on the contrary, if you are so convinced that God loves you regardless of your weaknesses, nothing can stop you from walking with Him because you know He is your stay. He is your righteousness and He has called you.

The conviction about the love of God was the secret of David, the man after God's own heart. David knew he was loved by God to the extent that even when God declared that He will punish him, he still said he wanted to fall into the hands of God because, "in Your hands there is mercy". This is the relationship we need to build with God so we can walk with Him with confidence and all reverence.

It is very important to understand that when it comes to the love of God, He is not dealing with us based on our performance. His love for us, His children, is a covenant love which is set and based on His never changing and never diminishing love for Christ. This is because we are in Christ and as long as He loves Christ, He also automatically loves us. If God can stop loving Christ then we are in trouble, but you and I know that that will never happen. Hence, we can be convinced that we are eternally loved. Let this sink deep into your heart. Meditate on it till it is all-natural to you. You know you are loved no matter what happens because you are in Christ.

The dimensions of the love of God

The love of God could be categorized into 3 main streams - breadth and length, the depth, and height (Ephesians 3:18). Let's take a look.

I believe that the dimensions of the love of God is mentioned in the scriptures to emphasize the truth that our salvation is not partial or only in some aspects of our lives but it covers every area and aspect of our lives; spirit soul, and body. The scripture says Jesus can save us to the uttermost.

Salvation is total and complete in every sense and the dimensions of the love of God make it clear that we are overshadowed by His love.

The breadth of God's love

This relates to what God's love covers and who and what aspects of our lives it covers. Scripture tells us that the love of God doesn't discriminate. It covers all people from every tribe, nation, and culture.

No country or nation is exempt from God's precious love. God has people in every nation (Rev. 5:9, 11, Col 3:11).

Nothing disqualifies you from receiving God's love unless you choose to reject the gift of salvation. The difference in race, ethnicity, social status, wealth etc. are not determinants of the love of God. There is absolutely no discrimination in God's love.

The breadth of God's love looks at how wide it reaches. According to scripture, God's love stretches beyond the bounds of all limitations.

No one can escape His unconditional love since He makes His sun shine upon all people, even those who do not know Him.

For the child of God, God's love stretches wide enough to cover us even into eternity. Remember and acknowledge that He cares about everything concerning you. Nothing is too big and nothing is too small for His attention. He can handle it all and He is very much interested.

The length of God's love

This refers to the endless character of God's love for you.

It relates to time. It answers the question of how long has He loved us and for how long will He continue to love us? When did it begin and when will it end?

God's love for the redeemed is eternal. He has loved us in Christ and this love will never end. He does not only love us here on earth but will continue His unfailing love towards us in eternity. What makes this even more amazing is the truth that He loved us before we were even created. He purposed to love us before the foundations of the world.

We are totally His idea, well thought of, totally loved and packaged with purpose. It is important to understand this so that when you are relating with God you can go to Him in confidence knowing He won't repel you. He knows what to do with you.

The "alwaysness" of His love is the strength of our confidence towards Him (Jer 31:3). Remember this; nothing can separate us from the love of God (Rom 8:38 – 39).

How long is God going to love you for? Forever!

The depths of His love

The depths of God's love are seen in what He did for us.

How deep does His love go? Well, what can be deeper than dying for your loved one?

"Greater love has no one than this than to lay down one's life for his friends" (John 15:13 NKJV).

God put on humanity and humbled Himself to come on earth to suffer and die for your sin and my sin. He did this for us! This was the beautiful exchange; He became sin that we might become righteousness. He died that we might live. He became poor that we might be rich.

The extent of his suffering at the cross shows the depths of His love for us. Look at Golgotha, look how He willingly surrendered to the will of the Father at Gethsemane just for us.

Indeed, greater love has no man than to lay down his life for another. He laid down His life for the church – His glorious bride.

The Bible says that for God so loved the world, that He gave his ONLY BEGOTTEN Son – to die for you! How deep is His love?

He suffered and died for you!

This is crazy love – He died with passion on purpose so you can be saved from sin, the world and the judgment of God against sin and sinners.

The depth of His love is further seen in the fact that He loved us in our mess – He didn't wait for us to be right. He died for us and made us right. Ephesians 2:4-9 explains the depths of His love:

> "But God, who is rich in mercy, because of His great love with which He loved us, even when we were dead in trespasses, made us alive together with

Christ (by grace you have been saved), and raised *us* up together, and made *us* sit together in the heavenly *places* in Christ Jesus, that in the ages to come He might show the exceeding riches of His grace in *His* kindness toward us in Christ Jesus. For by grace you have been saved through faith, and that not of yourselves; *it is* the gift of God, not of works, lest anyone should boast."

This is the depths of His love for you and me.

The height of His love

The height of God's love relates to where He is taking us to. It relates to our destiny. How we are supposed to end. This is glorious to even think about. Jesus in His prayer in John 17 asked God to take us where He is and to share in His glory.

He has made us joint-heirs with Christ (Romans 8:17).

My Pastor preached a message a while ago about the church and used the term *"Jasperisation."* This relates to the final appearance of Christ and the church at the end of the ages. The description of the church descending from heaven is shown as a mixture of Christ and man. This is the ultimate image and destination of the church; glorious just as Jesus is and immersed in Him. His plan is for our heart to beat as one.

We are told in 2 Corinthians 3:18 that as we behold Him in the word, we are changed into the same image as He is from glory to glory.

In Ephesians 2, The Apostle Paul stated clearly that when God raised Christ from the dead, He also raised us with Him and seated us with Him in the heavenly places. Mom, right now as a believer in Christ, you are seated with Him in the heavenly places!

That is your reality. Begin to walk in the consciousness of this truth and exercise your authority as a child of God.

All the benefits that come with salvation and glorification are yours as a child of God. Your destination is simply glory! He is daily transforming you to be just like Jesus as you continue to abide in Him. He is such a good God; He withholds nothing good from you. To think of the truth that He wants you to be like Jesus is so amazing. Blessed be His holy name. Your end is glory. The height of His love for you is glory!

Knowing the dimensions of the love of God is so important to everyone who wants to be a permanent dweller in the Secret Place because in challenging times, these truths will be the anchor that will keep you stable and unmovable.

Take time to soak yourself in the love of God by meditating on the scriptures that confirm these truths. Stay on them till you are convinced that absolutely nothing can separate you from the love of God. Abide in His love.

NEW CREATION REALITIES – IN HIM

The epistles especially reveal our new creation realities to us who are partakers of the New Covenant ratified by the shedding of the blood of Jesus. Apostle Paul took every opportunity to teach the various recipients of his letters who they have become in Christ and what has been made available to them in Him. Like them, when you accepted Christ as Lord, the blood of Jesus washed your past away, and from that very moment, you became a new creation in your spirit (2 Corinthians 5. 17). Although, all these promises are "yes and amen" in Christ (2 Corinthians 1:20), you will not be able to internalize them if you lack knowledge about them. By extension, not taking hold of them by faith will cause you to miss out on your rightful blessings in Christ. Knowing who you are in Christ is very vital to actualizing the promises of God here on earth.

In his book, *In Him*, Kenneth E. Hagin states the importance of searching the scriptures to find out all the "in Him" scriptures that explain who we are and what we have in Christ. These scriptures are then to become our meditation so they settle in our hearts before we can possess them by faith.

The Bible says that the whole of creation is awaiting the manifestation of the sons of God (Romans 8:19). Your manifestation to the world starts with knowing who and what Christ has made you be in Him, believe, it, confess it and then live it out. Make this all-important topic "in Him" one of your major meditation subjects. Meditate on these truths till they become the very source of your inspiration.

PRACTISING HIS PRESENCE

Apart from meditation, the other means for abiding in the Secret Place is through developing continual consciousness of God's presence with you and engaging in conversations with Him in our everyday activities. This is what many call "Practicing the Presence of God."

The aim of this exercise is basically to maintain consistent awareness of the presence of God with you. The Bible confirms to us in many scriptures that God is always with His children. One of the Biblical names of God is Jehovah Shammah; that means the God who is always present. Jesus also promised His continual presence with His disciples (Matthew 28:20).

Although the abiding presence of God is a Biblical fact, many do not recognize nor honour His presence in their lives, hence the minimal effects and manifestations of God in the lives of so many Christians. God will not force Himself on anyone.

The children of God have been given access to more of God but very few experience the riches of His glorious presence because we have not tapped into practising His presence. David said, "I have set the LORD always before me; Because *He is* at my right hand I shall not be moved." (Psalm 16:8 NKJV).

When we read or hear about the exploits of David, we may say he is so special, a man after God's own heart. I don't think he was more special than we are but he learnt how to harness the secret of practising God's presence, stewarding the presence and walking authentically before the Lord. This is available to us too if we can follow his example.

In Proverbs, God urges us to acknowledge Him in all our ways (Proverbs 3:6). The Creator of the universe wants to be engaged in everything we do. He is inviting us close. What a privilege and an honour it is for us to have such an audience with the King of Glory. Praise the Lord.

As you embrace the call into the Secret Place, remember to maintain an attitude of humility and awe towards God. Though He loves engaging with you, it is not for you to order Him about. He is not desperate nor in need of you. You are rather the desperate one who can't do without Him. Always bear this in mind so you can stay humble and attract more grace.

God simply wants to do life with you as a loving caring Father, Saviour, and Helper.

To obtain the maximum benefits of practising His presence, you must be intentional about it and invite God in every detail of your life.

Ask Him to go with you to work, school, or engage in any activity you are doing. Talk to Him about not only the 'big' things of life but even the seemingly insignificant things. He is interested in all. I found out that, when I do this, I make fewer mistakes, my day is more peaceful and much more productive.

BENEFITS OF PRACTISING THE PRESENCE OF GOD

Acknowledging God's presence at all times has countless benefits and when we begin to engage Him in conversation, we receive great wisdom, directions, and avoid evil and danger.

When you practice His presence, you are more effective in all you do and make fewer mistakes.

This exercise also shapes your character and opens you up to be used by God greatly.

You also enjoying knowing that God is close to you thus your heart is open to Him so you can hear Him well and respond to His instructions with an obedient heart, which causes many blessings to come your way while ensuring that you avoid many ills.

Building continual conversations with God will help you keep your mind stayed on Him all the time and enjoy His great peace (Isaiah 26:3).

You become bold and fearless in the face of danger because you are aware that you are not alone, God is with you.

It is reported that Smith Wigglesworth had an invisible friend who he constantly talked to about his life. He would talk to Him about what to preach, etc.

Brother Kenneth E. Hagan (as he is affectionately called by many) depicts a practical close relationship with God through his preaching. He often talks about conversations he had with God and sometimes in his prayers, it sounds like a simple conversation with a Good Friend.

The most popular person on this subject of practising His presence is Brother Lawrence – author of *The Practice of the Presence of God*. Though a simple monk working in a kitchen, Brother Lawrence learnt to just walk with God in such a beautifully practical way. We will discuss more of him later.

A SHORT TESTIMONY

Once I was talking with a colleague and at the same time, I was engaging God in my heart asking Him what He thinks about the subject we were talking about and what He would advise I say. I then heard in my heart, "why don't you just keep quiet and listen?" I then obeyed and listened to my colleague who opened up and poured out her heart to me regarding issues she was dealing with. This gave me the great honour of ministering to her. I would have missed this opportunity to be a blessing had I not engaged God in an internal conversation.

CONSECRATION

Another vital way to stay and remain in the Secret Place is to live a consecrated life. A Secret Place is a holy place and sin cannot stay there. This doesn't mean there is no hope for you if you fall because of a weakness. The blood of Jesus is always available to you if you will be quick to repent and deal with those sins and weights that easily ensnare you.

In the area of consecration, lets us look at three main areas that need to be our focus.

THE HEART

Stay consecrated in your heart so you can flow with God. The Bible urges us not to grieve or quench the Spirit. The sins of the heart which no one sees are dangerous and they can poison you. Sins of the heart left to fester will grieve the Holy Spirit and leaving them covered will affect your spiritual growth and development. In Hebrews 11, the Bible warns us to watch over ourselves so that no root of bitterness will spring up and defile many. Though not seen, the sins of the heart can defile you and even all those around you. Constantly search your heart and repent of any sin the Lord throws light on. Like my pastor (Rev Awo Antwi) says, "don't toy with sin otherwise, sin will toy with your destiny."

THE SOUL

The Bible talks about the prosperity of the soul which I understand to be the mind, will, and emotions.

These areas need to be brought under the control of the Holy Spirit to stay safe from worldly and sinful contaminations. The

Apostle Paul urges us to be changed by renewing our minds – that is to change the way we think and conform our thoughts to the thoughts of Christ.

You have the mind of Christ, and you are to put on Christ. Saturating your mind with the Word of God and keeping the right company would go a long way to help in this area.

In Hebrews 11 we are warned to avoid profanity like Esau – who sold his birth right. He didn't value his place in God. You must, therefore, watch your attitude so you don't undermine the valuable things of God.

THE BODY

You have to stay consecrated in your body by keeping pure from sexual immorality and every form of physical impurity such as debauchery, idolatry, and the like. Your body is the temple of God and must be holy and well-kept, in good health, and honourable in presentation. You are to present your body as a living sacrifice, holy and acceptable to the Lord.

9

FRIENDSHIP WITH THE HOLY SPIRIT

All the above discussion about remaining in the Secret Place will not be possible without the Holy Spirit. If you try, you may be able to produce some form of lifeless religion void of the life of God.

Friendship with the Holy Spirit is so vital to staying in the Secret Place of the Most High. He is the power of God that is at work in you, for you, through you, and with you.

It is vital to get to know Him.

Without getting too deep into the theology on the subject of the Trinity, I will just mention that the Holy Spirit is the third Person of the Trinity. He is therefore not "it," but "He." He feels moves, senses, and has all the characteristics of a personality. As the source of all power, you have to develop a good, strong relationship with Him.

ENGAGE THE HOLY SPIRIT

As you meditate, ask the Holy spirit to throw light on the scripture. Expect Him to speak to you and as you read and think about the word great light will flood your soul. Don't get frustrated when you don't hear anything. Repeat the process and you will soon start receiving the ministry of the Holy Spirit in your meditation effortlessly.

How to build a good relationship with the Holy Spirit

Honour

The Holy Spirit is God and so He likes order. He will not stay in a place where He is dishonoured or where there is no respect for any God-ordained authority. It is vital to honour Him as God if you want to build a good relationship with Him.

Start your day with Him by honouring Him with gratitude and a 'good morning Holy Spirit' to set you on a good track towards building that relationship.

Authenticity

The Holy Spirit doesn't like fake. Be yourself and express yourself honestly to Him all the time. Never lie to Him regardless of the situation. It is safer to speak the truth to Him than hide behind a lie.

Music

The Holy Spirit seems to like music for some reason; especially, when it comes from a pure and sincere heart of worship. His presence is often manifested in an atmosphere of worship. Singing to Him will draw Him to you. I love singing a lot because when I do, I sense Him so strongly. A worship-filled atmosphere is a great place to encounter Him

Consecration

He is the Holy Spirit; avoid un-holiness so you can be friends. If you fall, confess quickly and repent. If you make excuses for sin and stay in it, you are only asking Him to leave you, because He just can't cohabit with sin.

DON'T GRIEVE OR QUENCH HIM.

Grieving Him means making Him sad. Sin, disobedience, faithlessness, dishonour, pride, greed, and all other forms of evil can grieve Him. Sometimes it may not even be a clear sin but whenever you do, say, or think something that He prompted you not to do, you grieve Him. He is sensitive and tender so you must walk with Him circumspectly. A rich relationship with the Spirit is glorious.

10

ACTIVATING THE BLESSINGS IN PSALM 91

THE PLACE OF DECLARATIONS

In the preceding chapters, we have learnt about what the Secret Place is, how to dwell there and how to ensure we remain there continually.

We have also learnt that Secret Place is a place of refuge and blessing which comes with the human responsibility in activating the blessings and protection available to us. This is the secret we must all learn if we are to release all the spiritual blessings we are blessed with in the heavenly places.

The secret for releasing the blessing for those dwelling in the Secret Place is hidden in the words in verse 2, *"I will say..."*

Notice that right after this statement, the blessing kicks in. Faith declarations release and activate the blessing.

Dwelling in the Secret Place through maintaining a living thriving connection with God as discussed above are great, but in order to see the manifestation of the blessing, you must activate or release it with your words through declarations of faith. This is the same principle of faith that is required for salvation: believe in your heart and confess with your mouth. It is also the same principle for living the Christian life; we walk and live by faith. We believe what God's word has said and we declare it to see it manifest in our lives.

In the realm of the spirit, words are powerful. Words are creative so when you utter what you truly believe in your heart, you are giving life and matter to it; it is just a matter of time and you will see what you have declared with your eyes.

Jesus made this spiritual principle clear in Mark 11:22-24, "So Jesus answered and said to them, "Have faith in God. For assuredly, I say to you, whoever says to this mountain, 'Be removed and be cast into the sea,' and does not doubt in his heart, but believes that those things he says will be done, he will have whatever he says. Therefore I say to you, whatever things you ask when you pray, believe that you receive *them,* and you will have *them..*"

As you take time to abide through prayer, the study of the word and meditation, you also need to move on to the confession of the word in order to release the blessing, or as Gloria Copeland put it, "We take it by faith." Remember, "faith works by speaking" (Rev Dr David Antwi). You can refer to Proverbs 12:14, Proverbs 18:20, Joshua 1:8, and Romans 10:9 which authenticate the power of confessing what you believe. These scriptures highlight the truth that life and death are in the power of the tongue. You create life or death, good or bad, with your own words so be mindful of what you say.

Your words are powerful; especially, words of faith, so release the blessing with the words of your mouth. Agreeing with God and speaking His word will produce good and release his blessings over you, your family, and any situation you may be going through.

With this understanding, you can be sure of the following blessings as a permanent dweller in the Secret Place of the Most High. Why not personalise this psalm and declare it regularly over your life:

I dwell in the Secret Place of the Most High. I abide under the shadow of the Almighty
I say of the Lord, He is my refuge
Surely He shall deliver me from the snare of the fowler
***And* from the perilous pestilence.**

Gloria Boakye

He shall cover me with His feathers,
And under His wings I shall take refuge;
His truth *shall be my* shield and buckler.
I shall not be afraid of the terror by night,
Nor of the arrow *that* flies by day,
Nor of the pestilence *that* walks in darkness,
Nor of the destruction *that* lays waste at noonday.
A thousand may fall at my side,
And ten thousand at my right hand;
But it shall not come near me.
Only with my eyes shall I look,
And see the reward of the wicked.
Because I have made the Lord, *who is* my refuge,
Even the Most High, my dwelling place,
No evil shall befall me,
Nor shall any plague come near my dwelling;
For He shall give His angels charge over me,
To keep me in all my ways.
In *their* hands, they shall bear me up,
Lest I dash my foot against a stone.
I shall tread upon the lion and the cobra,
The young lion and the serpent I shall trample underfoot.'
Because I has set my love upon Him, therefore He will deliver me;
He will set me on high because I have known His name.
I shall call upon Him, and He will answer him;
He *will be* with me in trouble;
He will deliver me and honour him.
With long life, He will satisfy me,
And show me His salvation. (Psalm 91:1-16 - personalised)

This is so heart-warming indeed. Blessed be His holy name

11

WHAT IF YOU FAIL?

Looking honestly at all the above discussion, the concept of dwelling in the Secret Place may probably come across as a rather lofty ambition considering the normal lifestyle of the average believer today.

Can you abide in the Secret Place and experience all these blessings? This sounds like a life of perfection! Who is perfect after all? These may be some of the questions that would pop up in your mind. I will attempt to deal with these questions in the remaining chapter of the book.

I don't doubt the possibility of abiding in the Secret Place because God will never ask us to do something He has not equipped us to do.

The question of perfection, on the other hand, can be discussed because we are all "work in progress." Perfection will only be attained when we see Jesus face to face. In the meantime, we keep working at it, we keep striving towards the mark for the prize of the upward calling.

Thus, the question is not the absence of failure but what we do with it.

I am certain you are likely to experience failure at some point in your effort at abiding in the Secret Place. I have failed many times and as I am currently writing this, I am not in my best state as pertains to abiding in the Secret Place. Though my routine of prayer remains, it is not always easy staying focused especially when things are not going according to plan.

What do you do in times like that? Faith! This is when you and I need our faith the most. We must keep believing for the things we hope for and maintain our confidence in the God.

In difficult times when you are not really in the flow for whatever reason, don't break your connection with God. Stay in touch with Him no matter what is going on.

This is where the *"Gethsemane principle,"* real authenticity before the Lord, comes to play. Let us look at how Jesus handled difficult challenging circumstances that could have pushed Him out of the place of God or the will of God.

JESUS IN GETHSEMANE

On the night that He was betrayed, Jesus did not run from God when confronted with the challenge of facing the cross and rejection from His disciples and ultimately, momentary separation from the Father. He was about to bear the sin of the world and become sin, which meant the Father had to forsake Him for that moment. This was so unbearable for Jesus to imagine. It was a real challenge because Jesus couldn't bear life without the Father, not even for a moment!

In this predicament, Jesus run to the Father and opened up to Him in all honesty and sincerity with a yielded heart. The result of such openness and authenticity before God was an abundance of grace and strength supplied to Him to enable Him to finish the task of the salvation of man. We must follow Jesus' example and walk before the Lord with all authenticity in challenging times. His grace will abound to us, too and we can finish our assignment well just as Jesus did (Matthew 26:36-46).

King David, one of the greatest Old Testament characters who loved the presence of God, had several failures but that didn't stop him. He kept going back to God, falling into the arms of His loving, merciful Father because he knew God will never give up on him (2 Samuel 24:14).

OBSTACLES TO REMAINING IN THE SECRET PLACE

Let's discuss a few of the obstacles that may hinder your pursuit of staying in the Secret Place.

THE FLESH

"Flesh" refers to our human abilities outside of God. It is what we are without Christ. Scripture commands us to bring the flesh under subjection (1 Corinthians 9:27). This is not attained by beating ourselves but by strengthening our spirit man. Prayers (especially praying in the spirit), the study of the word, meditation, and fellowship with the saints are key means of strengthening the spirit and weakening the flesh (Galatians 5:16, Jude 1:20, Proverbs 4:22, John 6:63, 1 Thessalonians 5:11)

Discipline your mind to keep it on God's word because the output of your life is a result of your dominant thoughts (Proverbs 23:7). Easier said than done, I know! Having lived most of your life in a way that may be contrary to what you want to do now, it will take some time and effort to make the necessary changes. Don't be discouraged if you fail. Pull yourself together and do it again and again. Sometimes, you can fast to intensify your resolve and call on God to help you.

Your source of inspiration for right living is always the Word of God and Jesus is our ultimate example. When Jesus was tempted in the flesh in the wilderness, He defeated the devil with the Word of God (Luke 4:1-13). You can also overcome by declaring the Word back when tempted by the flesh. We can boldly declare that you can do all things through Christ who strengthens you (Philippians 4:13).

CHALLENGES AND CARES OF LIFE

Challenges have a way of sweeping you off your feet if you are not steadfast and unmovable in the Lord.

It is easy to believe and feel God's presence when everything is nice and cosy around you, but when the unexpected and unpleasant happen, you may begin to doubt God. As you strive to handle the challenges in your strength, you may lose consciousness of God's presence.

Many Believers have fallen into spiritual sleep or abandoned their faith altogether because a challenge occurred. This ought not to be so. I understand that it can be discouraging when you have done all you can to maintain a vital connection with God only for tragedy to hit or for things to go bad. In times like that, your faith can be challenged but I will encourage you not to throw away your confident trust in God.

"Do not cast away your confidence, which has great reward. For you have need of endurance, so that after you have done the will of God, you may receive the promise" (Hebrews 10:35-36).

Develop yourself so much that in times of trouble your default response would be more of "run to God" instead of a "run away from God." Maintain the presence of God in your life, fill your heart with the Word of God! That way when circumstances "squeeze" you, it is the Word that will come out and the Word will only lead you to God.

Troubles are not necessarily a sign that God is not with you. Jesus promises us challenges. However, these are not meant to destroy you but to make you stronger (John 6:33).

Apostle Paul emphasized this truth when he encouraged us to count it all joy when we go through diverse kinds of tribulations (James 1:2-3).

For a child of God who loves God, difficulties cannot destroy you. They cannot cancel God's plan for you but rather work together for your good (Romans 8:28).

When you are tested by challenges, don't give up but lean in closer to God and ask Him what level He is taking you next. Although Psalm 91 promises you blessings and protection from evil, it doesn't say that trouble will never come; rather, **God promises to be with you in trouble and to deliver you from them.**

Be of good cheer therefore, your trials will not last. Keep your eyes on Jesus and He will deliver you. I know He will because He does it for me all the time and He is no respecter of persons. Expect Him to deliver you as you remain steady, abiding in the Secret Place.

ATTACKS FROM THE DEVIL

The devil knows you will be out of his reach if you become a permanent dweller in the Secret Place so he will not just watch you go; he will fight you. Don't just sit and take his ugly punches.

Fight back fully armed with all the weapons that the Lord has given you. In 1 Peter 5:8, we are admonished to be sober and vigilant because we have an enemy who is always looking for a victim to devour. That will never be you or me in the mighty name of Jesus! Amen! Let us look at the victory strategy provided in 1 Peter 5:8-9 to adhere to it to avoid and overcome the cunning devices of the devil:

Be Sober

This means be clear-headed. Think straight. Don't be clouded with worry, uncertainty and doubt. This is so important because the main battleground where the enemy attacks is in your mind. As a mother, you must be diligent at managing your thoughts and conform them to the Word of God. Take charge over every thought by deciding what you hear, see, and say because that will be your focus and that is what will occupy your mind.

In Romans 12:2 we are admonished to renew our minds. That means our thoughts must agree with the Word of God. Get into the Word of God and deliberately ensure that what you are hearing, seeing and saying agree with God's word.

Pay close attention to the thoughts that pop up in your mind and ensure that those thoughts that are contrary to God's word are rejected and replaced immediately with what God has said.

Instead of fighting negative thoughts with positive thoughts, speak the Word of God against every negative thought that comes into your mind. For instance, if an evil thought enters your mind and tells you, "you are you going to be sick" or "something bad is going to happen," don't accept that thought and don't try to fight it by thinking positive thoughts. That won't work. Rather, speak out what God has said about your health. Declare by faith that you are healed by the stripes of Jesus and that you will live to declare the works of the Lord. As you continue to declare the word, faith will rise in your heart and that negative thought will flee from you (Mark 11:23).

Be Vigilant

This means watching out for danger and opportunities. Jesus advised us to be wise like serpents and be harmless like doves (Romans 10:16). Be aware that there is an enemy out there who wants to steal from you, kill your destiny, potentials, opportunities, and life, and a foe who wants to utterly destroy every good thing in your life (John 10:10).

There is a wicked devil out there and though you don't have to get obsessed with him, it is very foolish to live as if he doesn't exist. Live watchfully. Mind what you open up to, where you go and who you associate with.

Don't walk about blindly but be wise in all your dealings. Listen and obey your spirit because God will talk to you through your spirit. If you are not sure about something, pause and pray about it.

It is important to emphasize that you do not have to walk in fear but rather walk boldly and wisely. Faith is your victory (1 John

5:4). Believe that greater is He who is in you than the devil who is after you.

Take your right place and exercise your authority in Christ over and against all the powers of the enemy and nothing shall by any means hurt you in the mighty name of Jesus (1 John 4:4, Ephesians 2:6, Revelations 12:11).

Another important side of vigilance is not only to watch for danger, but also watch out for opportunities to do good and impact lives positively. Don't be so preoccupied with staying safe that you miss your opportunities of making a difference, increasing, and expanding your righteous influence in the places God has planted you. God wants you to do well, and success is a major tool for victory.

Stand against the wiles of the enemy, fully clothed with the whole amour of God. This is to ensure you are properly equipped for battle and not unnecessarily exposed to the elements (Ephesians 6:10-18).

As you adhere to these instructions, you can walk with confidence knowing that your weapons are not carnal but mighty through God to demolish and destroy every stronghold and satanic opposition in your way! You are more than a conqueror in Him!

Forgiveness

When we talk about forgiveness, it presupposes that there is an offence, a hurt, a difficult or a painful situation or incident against yourself or another. It is never an easy subject to discuss because there is always real pain involved. This is never an easy thing. For example, you can suffer major heartache if you are betrayed by a loved and sometimes the damage can be very serious. It is never an easy thing to deal with naturally. It is important for you to acknowledge this fact before you can do anything about the problem.

Don't use the usual "Christianese" (common Christian jargons), the "all is well" talk by some Christians who do not face the realities of their issues, and never deal with them- meaning they don't experience the total freedom that comes from Christ.

The Bible never told us to deny the existence of problems but to overcome them with power and grace. First, acknowledge the fact that you are hurt or offended. Then begin the scriptural process of dealing with the offence which is through forgiveness.

Jesus gave clear instructions on dealing with offences. We are not to pretend nothing has happened and just keep the pain in. This will only lead to eventual "explosion". Jesus said if a brother or sister offends you go talk to them about it and deal with it. He gives stages to go through including involving others and the church if the situation is proving stubborn.

According to the instruction in the Lord's prayer, regardless of the response of the offender, we are to forgive to also qualify for forgiveness from God. I believe the process of going through the motions of dealing with the hurt though helpful, may clear the air and also somehow free the offender.

On your part, if you want to please God and stay in His will then forgiveness is not optional for you. You just have to do it. I understand that in some cases, this can be difficult but with God all things are possible. I like to follow Jesus' examples of dealing with situations. On the cross, Jesus asked God to forgive the very people who were killing Him.

Offence is poisonous. You are only hurting yourself if you hold on to offences. I recently learnt about the scientific proof of people being entangled.

According to Dr Caroline Leaf, when you hold on to an offence, you are giving too much power and control to the offender and they are more or less controlling your life, you are not free.

Just let it go and let God take over.

Forgiving people does not make them right, it only makes you free.

Offence will rob you of the presence of God. You can't continue to stay in the Secret Place if you hold offences in your heart. I don't think it is worth losing the glorious presence of God because you prefer to hold on to a toxic offence.

Unforgiveness is a blocker of the presence. You are to abide in the Secret Place of the Highest, then you are required to forgive everyone.

Get up again from a fall

The preceding points emphasizes the need for holiness and purity if we are to abide in the Secret Place of the Most High.

In our humanity, sometimes we fall. You may lose your consciousness of God's presence if the weaknesses of the flesh ever lead to a fall and if not handled right. In 1 John 1:8-9, the Bible says: "we say that we have no sin, we deceive ourselves, and the truth is not in us. If we confess our sins, He is faithful and just to forgive us *our* sins and to cleanse us from all unrighteousness"

Note that this scripture was written to Christians. That means that although as born-again Christians, we are not sinners, there may be times that we may fall into sin. When/if that happens, we are to quickly confess our sins and be cleansed by the blood of Jesus.

If you happen to fall into sin, don't wallow in it nor stay in the place of regret.

Get hold on the Word of God and confess and forsake the sin quickly. The longer you stay in guilt, the more entangled you become.

Pray to God for forgiveness and get back into fellowship. His blood took away your sins and His grace will cover you. Don't stay in the dark, run back into the loving arms of the Father and be restored.

12

BIBLICAL CASE STUDIES

Joseph, Moses, Joshua, David, the Apostle Paul, and of course our ultimate example, Jesus Himself, shine bright as our Biblical examples of dwellers in the Secret Place.

With the exception of Jesus, all the others were people who were bridled with many failures but navigated their path into His presence and maintained a solid relationship with God, thereby giving them a good report. Let us glean from their life stories.

JOSEPH (GENESIS 37 – 45)

Joseph was the beloved son of Jacob/Israel. He was much loved by his father but hated, mistreated and eventually sold by his blood brothers. I can't imagine anything more painful than betrayal by those who are supposed to love you.

Yet in all his trails, the Bible tells us that Joseph maintained his purity and loyalty to God. Even at the most opportune occasions to make himself great (through an evil means), he held on to his faith and resisted the temptation (Genesis 39:9). He chose to suffer for righteousness sake instead of accepting comfort at the expense of his conscience and purity towards God.

Amid all His trials, the Bible says that "but God was with him" (Genesis 39:2, 21).

Joseph walked in the consciousness of God's presence and so was led and guided by God in every way.

Eventually, with God's help, he became the prime minister of Egypt and through him, his family and the nation of Israel were preserved.

Joseph's ability to stay pure amid difficulties and trials was hinged on his relationship with God. He valued God and His ways and cherished God's law (Word) in his heart. Consequently, he had the strength to stand and to stay pure to the end. He understood that his circumstances were orchestrated by God, a great proof of the grace of God and deep intimacy (Genesis 50:20).

Joseph constantly spoke highly of His God to all he encountered. He stated boldly before Pharaoh that God was his source and that understanding comes from the Lord (Genesis 41:16).

If Joseph could maintain such a consciousness of God and stay loyal and faithful to God in the most opposing circumstances, so can we because the grace of God abounds even more to us now through Christ.

MOSES (EXODUS 2 - 34)

Moses is one of the people in the Bible that I greatly admire for various reasons. I think it is because of his heart; very tender, caring, and graceful indeed (Numbers 12:3, Exodus 32:11).

Right from his birth, Pharaoh attempted to wipe him out but his destiny was preserved by the sovereign hand of God. God sent him into the very house of the one who was seeking to destroy him to be nurtured and trained. Very interesting indeed. God is not limited; He will even use your enemies to fulfil His purposes for your life if you stay in His will.

Moses's encounter with God was first at the burning bush. When God asked him to go get His people out of Egypt, Moses had a hearty talk with God about his weaknesses, fears and inabilities (Exodus 4:13).

I like the sincere conversation that went on between Moses and God. The honest but reverent conversation is what we are also called into. In the process of attempting to convince Pharaoh to let the people of God go, Moses would go back to God over and over again, inquiring of Him for direction. I like his honesty when he spoke with God. With all reverence, he spoke his heart with honesty.

"So Moses returned to the LORD and said, "Lord, why have You brought trouble on this people? Why *is* it You have sent me?" (Exodus 5:22)

He was conscious of the power and guidance of God. He depended on God throughout the process and He steadily built his trust and reliance on God, and He never failed him.

At the Red Sea, it had to take one who knew God at a certain level and depth to trust that the sea will part for them to walkthrough

"Then Moses stretched out his hand over the sea, and the LORD caused the sea to go *back* by a strong east wind all that night and made the sea into dry *land,* and the waters were divided" (Exodus 14:21).

In the wilderness, Moses experienced many dynamic encounters as proof of an intimate walk with God - talking to God face to face for forty days, and receiving the ten commandments, among others. Moses became so accustomed to the presence that he wouldn't venture anything without the presence of God going with him.

"Then he said to Him, "If Your Presence does not go *with us,* do not bring us up from here" (Exodus 33:15).

Eventually, when God told Moses that he wouldn't go to the Promised Land because of his disobedience at the waters of Meribah (Numbers 20:2-13), though painful, we see Moses's meek acceptance of his fate and his willingness to prepare Joshua to take over from him (Deuteronomy 3:28).

In the end, Moses didn't go to the Promised Land which he had worked for, but God was still with him as a friend.

Following God's instructions, Moses prepared Joshua to take over from him. He did this willingly by yielding to the Lord.

Through Joshua, Moses's assignment of taking the children of Israel to the Promised Land was fulfilled.

"Now the Lord said to Moses: "Go up into this Mount Abarim, and see the land which I have given to the children of Israel. And when you have seen it, you also shall be gathered to your people, as Aaron your brother was gathered. For in the Wilderness of Zin, during the strife of the congregation, you rebelled against My command to hallow Me at the waters before their eyes." (These *are* the waters of Meribah, at Kadesh in the Wilderness of Zin.)

Then Moses spoke to the Lord, saying: "Let the Lord, the God of the spirits of all flesh, set a man over the congregation, who may go out before them and go in before them, who may lead them out and bring them in, that the congregation of the Lord may not be like sheep which have no shepherd." Numbers 27:12-17 NKJV.

At the end of His life, though God didn't change His mind about Moses going to the Promised Land, He stayed with him and even personally buried Moses.

"Then Moses went up from the plains of Moab to Mount Nebo, to the top of Pisgah, which is across from Jericho. And the Lord showed him all the land of Gilead as far as Dan, all Naphtali and the land of Ephraim and Manasseh, all the land of Judah as far as the Western Sea, the South, and the plain of the Valley of Jericho, the city of palm trees, as far as Zoar. Then the Lord said to him, "This *is* the land of which I swore to give Abraham, Isaac, and Jacob, saying, 'I will give it to your descendants.' I have caused you to see *it* with your eyes, but you shall not cross over there." So Moses the servant of the Lord died there in the land of Moab, according to the word of the Lord. And He buried him in a valley in the land of Moab, opposite Beth Peor; but no one knows his grave to this day. Moses *was* one hundred and twenty years old when he died. His eyes were not dim nor his natural vigour diminished" (Deuteronomy 34:1-7).

Moses had a beautiful relationship with God. Even though Moses's weakness of anger cost him the prize of going into the Promised Land, God never left him. They stayed close to the end.

JOSHUA (THE BOOK OF JOSHUA)

In modern terms, I will call Joshua a very 'hard follower' of Moses. He was a faithful and loyal servant and protégée of Moses. It is not surprising that the mantle of leadership fell on him to finish Moses's job of taking the people of Israel into the promised land.

Joshua loved the presence so much that he continued to linger in the house of God and His presence even when everyone had left (Exodus 33:11).

He was just drawn to God. His proximity and service to Moses earned him the privilege of gleaning from the field of grace and presence that Moses the servant of God enjoyed.

Joshua learnt that success was a function of God's power, not natural strength and so he didn't try to train harder or get better contacts when he was tasked with the enormous responsibility of leading the people of Israel. He received his directions and strategies from the Lord just as Moses did (Joshua 1:1-10).

Walking closely with God in obedience enabled Joshua to victoriously overcome all his enemies and achieve 100% success in his leadership.

He knew and feared God to the core and walked in obedience to all of His commandments. God also honoured His word and gave him total victory and success just as He promised to do (Joshua 1:8-10).

Just like Joshua, as we look unto Jesus the author and finisher of our faith, we will also fulfil our destinies to full capacity, in the mighty name of Jesus (Hebrews 12:2).

KING DAVID

King David is another one of my most favourite characters in the Bible for a couple of reasons. I love his life of worship and dependence on God.

He is referred to as the man after God's own heart.

He is a great example of a person abiding continually in the Secret Place and walking before the Lord with authenticity.

As evidenced in scripture, David had many flaws but what is most striking about David is how he never lost sight of God's presence with him. Even when he felt unworthy and deserving of punishment, he acknowledged the mercies of God and asked to fall into the hands of God for judgment because he knew that in His arms, he would find mercy.

David had a sweet relationship with God. May the Lord draw us into Himself in such a manner that nothing can ever make us think we can't approach Him.

If David, who didn't have Christ had such a wonderful relationship with God then we can even do better, for, in Christ, sin is history.

Nothing can separate us from God's love, we can go to Him anytime for in Him we live and move and have our being.

The Apostle Paul

In the early years of my Christian life, before I was significantly transformed from the world, I didn't like the Apostle Paul because he sounded too strict and seemed to be against makeup, fashion, and good looks which were, and indeed still are, my thing.

I thought he was against women dressing up and looking good.

Of course, this is absurd but that is what I thought then. What a silly lie that was!

Thank God for good teachings and avid study of God's word.

My eyes are now open and I love the Apostle Paul! Hallelujah!

What a life of dedication and love for God he lived. He is a true example of a sold-out disciple. His life of total abandonment through challenging and extreme circumstances is one that can only happen as a result of a continual consciousness of the realities of heaven and the glories of God's presence and treasures.

To the Apostle Paul, heaven was as real as earth and he would choose heaven any day. As a result of a lifestyle of total consciousness of the Lord, he was able to go through thick and thin to finish his assignment here on earth with joy.

Abiding in the Secret Place was normal to Paul and we can learn to do the same because the same grace that enabled him is available to us, too.

THE LORD JESUS CHRIST

"Jesus Christ Is Perfect Theology," said Bill Johnson. Everything about Christianity is embodied in the person of Jesus Christ. He is our ultimate example of everything godly.

Jesus lived perfectly and constantly in the presence of God.

He said He only did what He saw the Father do.

Looking and learning from Jesus will help us live our lives in the Secret Place.

Though Jesus is God, when He was on earth He operated as a man dependent on the Spirit of God just as we are. Therefore, His example of intimacy with God is a great example for us.

The depths of His intimacy with the Father was most vivid at the cross when he cried out, "My God, My God, why have You forsaken Me" (Matthew 27:46). He couldn't bear being without the Father for a moment. We must be the same. His presence should be everything to us and we must labour to enter there and stay there no matter the cost.

His grace is available to us and it is also sufficient for us. Let us all embrace this call into the Secret Place. It is a beautiful place and a place of safety.

OTHER CONTEMPORARY STORIES

Apart from biblical examples, many have also lived this glorious life in God's presence and their lives are a great encouragement and hope to us that we can also do it. Amongst such people are Brother

Lawrence (Author of *The Practice of the Presence of God*) John G Lake, Brother Kenneth E Hagin and many more. For the sake of time, I will only discuss Brother Lawrence.

Brother Lawrence

Brother Lawrence is popularly known for his book, *The Practice of the Presence of God*.

He was a monk working in the kitchen of a monastery but he became popular because he was known to be a carrier of God's presence. Although, he didn't have the wealth of this world, he was rich in glory and so many sought an audience with him, so they could be blessed by the manifest presence of God that Brother Lawrence carried.

To Brother Lawrence, there was no difference between prayer time and work time for he was always with Him. He lived out Psalm 73:28, God's clossness indeed was his goodness.

Brother Lawrence made the practice of God's presence so practical and relatable to everyday ordinary life so that God was in everything he did.

To Brother Lawrence, worship was not confined to a chapel.

He worshipped and talked with God anywhere and everywhere. He walked in the reality of God's continual and abiding presence. God was always close to him.

This is real Christianity. We are to be Christians all the time not just on Sundays or only in church settings. Every minute and every hour of our lives must be lived as Christians with the consciousness and involvement of our Lord.

Conclusion

It has been an honour sharing with you on the Secret Place. As I conclude, I will encourage you to do two things: stay committed and stay consistent in your pursuit of God.

Commitment is what establishes a thing. Abiding in the Secret Place is an upward climb which requires effort. The effort is that of faith; the good fight of faith, accompanied by a continual gaze upon Jesus, the author and finisher of our faith. This is the only way to stay strong and motivated because as the author John C Maxwell said, "the journey to the top is up-hill all the way."

It may seem lonely at times because many people are not willing to pay the price for the call into the Secret Place. The journey upward, unlike the bottom, is seldom crowded, there is always room for you. You require the companionship of the Holy Spirit and total trust in God to keep going.

Stay focused and keep your eyes on Christ.

The Secret Place of the Most High is the best and safest place to ABIDE – to STAY, to REMAIN. The author of Psalm 91 (Moses) knew by experience that God's presence is the safest place and so he wouldn't attempt anything without the assurance of His glorious presence going with him.

In Christ, you have access into the Secret Place for in Him you live, move and have your being.

As a mother, it is a privilege to abide in the Secret Place because you are assured of a beautiful relationship with God; and your destiny and that of your children and family are safely placed under His protection and power.

I humbly invite you to take this journey into His Presence. It may not happen immediately but don't stop pursuing Him with all your heart.

In the Secret Place, you get to know God experientially. The more of Him you know, the more you desire and the quest never ends. The Secret Place is a satisfying place where the greatest longings and desires of your heart are fulfilled.

Come on into the Secret Place of the Most High. Abide under the shadow of the Almighty and blossom under His shade where you are supernaturally protected and eternally glorified.

Be Inspired! Start the Journey today! You won't regret you ever did! I look forward to hearing your testimony.

About the Author

Mrs. Gloria Boakye is a mother of 3 girls and happily married to Pastor Joseph Boakye.

Gloria is committed to pursuing the presence of God and living from His presence as a lifestyle. She is a lover of God and believes that Christians are to live a life totally immersed in the presence of the God who is interested in every detail of our lives.

Gloria believes that real joy and fulfilment can only be found when we live with the heart of God and is therefore committed to sharing this passion with others in a practical workable way.

Gloria serves actively in her church; Kharis Ministries in diverse capacities.

Gloria is driven by her passion to see mothers and young women live up to their potentials in God. This passion is what spurs her on to offer a helping hand of hope, encouragement, and inspiration to all she encounters to aid them in becoming all that God has ordained them to be.

Gloria holds a Master's degree in Business Administration, is currently running her own thriving Business and also works as an Administrator.

Printed in the United States
By Bookmasters